TRADING FOOT BETFAIR
HELPING YOU TO BECOME A WINNING TRADER
BY
THE MENTAL TRADER

https://twitter.com/thementaltrader
© Paul Watson 2022

All rights reserved. No part of this publication may be reproduced in any form or by any means without the prior permission in writing of the author and publisher.

Please note it is the authors intention to be as accurate in fact, detail and comment as possible. No guarantees of any kind regarding earnings are offered, due to the nature of the book and its intent. Entering trades is done solely at the risk of the individual bettor or trader and the author cannot in any way be held responsible. The publisher cannot be held responsible for any error in detail, accuracy or judgement whatsoever.

Acknowledgements.
I would like to thank the following for their help, their knowledge, their support and inspiration,

whether they are aware of it or not. Without them this book would not have been possible.

Wayne Morgan, Mike Cruickshank, Steve Brown, Caan Berry, Peter Webb, Kevin Laverick, Tony Hargraves (aka The Badger), Lee Mayne, John Preddy, Garry Scullion, John Palmer, Paul Eagles, Scott McFarland, Anne Smith, Susan Hook, Clive Keeling, John Douglas, Andrew David.

Thanks also goes to the countless traders across various social media groups that I've had the immense honour to have been involved with, and who have all helped make this book a reality.

Introduction.

Before we get to the meat and potatoes of finding our selections. Let me tell you what this book is not.
It will not teach you how to use the Betfair Exchange. Neither will it show you how to place a back or lay bet. You need to have a basic understanding of the Betfair interface and be able to place both back and lay bets on selections. There are many online tutorials that will explain the basics for you if you are totally new to it all. You don't need to know much more than backing and laying to get started.
While writing this book, I am attempting to describe things as if we were both sat in the same room. I'll strive to be as clear and easy to understand as possible.

Also understand, we are traders, not gamblers. We take advantage of the flow of money, of supply and demand and we trade using the price movements either before or after an event.
Ideally we back high and lay low, or the reverse and exit to our advantage as soon as we can.
If that is not possible due to the way the game is going, we exit as quickly as we can, so keeping our losses small.
We cannot win every trade, that is impossible,

but we can always be ready to exit or go for more gains by keeping a close eye on the match stats. Gamblers don't have this option. They either win or lose. Traders have other avenues. There is always the option to cut a trade short to minimise a loss, take a full stake loss, break even, or take the profit that we are happy with. We can do this with staking too. There's no need to go in pre-match with the full stake. We can always drip in our cash, or decide not to enter at all if we see that the in-play stats are not showing promise. Gamblers are happy to place a small stake in the hope of a large return. Most do nothing to mitigate that loss. It is a black or white result. Either a win or a loss.

The more savvy punters will have a wager on a particular outcome with a bookie and perhaps place the opposite bet when the opportunity presents itself on Betfair, so as to guarantee a profit or break even. If the team they have backed take the lead, that will be an option and is much more sensible than crossing fingers and hoping the score stays as it is for the full match. Traders take that a stage further and are looking to use the exchange exclusively and take over the role of the bookie altogether, by determining their own odds from the statistics that are available, making their own call on what prices are correct and acting accordingly.

Traders will always use discipline and patience,

to separate themselves from the majority of other punters.

A wise man once said that trading is simply the patient trader making and taking money from impatient ones.

Trading isn't a fast way to make money. It is very easy to place a trade and make a profit in the short term, but to be successful for any length of time, means commitment and for most people, a paradigm shift regarding profiting from betting. If it were as easy as some of the charlatans online would have us believe, every man and his dog would be doing it.
It can be learned. New thought patterns can be cultivated and long term success can be yours. Just don't expect it to happen overnight.

Do you need specialist trading software to succeed? The short answer is no, not in the beginning. While it certainly does help you to get your trades into the market quicker, and you will probably be using it a lot as you progress, in the beginning it isn't necessary. It makes life easier. It doesn't make your trades any better. You need to learn how to do that yourself.

Within these pages there are 14 Football Trading

Strategies.
Each strategy has its own Entry and Exit points, and it would be wise to make them hard and fast rules in the beginning. As you become more proficient, you may find you adapt them here and there, according to your own particular preferences, but that comes with experience. For now stick to the rules I have laid out.

At the end of each strategy, where necessary I've included what to look out for to help you in finding your own selections.
Every strategy has been tried and tested over many years and is clearly laid out and easy to understand.
From the basic LTD (updated Lay The Draw,) to the more involved
Correct Score markets, to using simple dutching techniques. All can be very profitable when combined with solid, statistically sound selections.

You won't need 14 strategies. You will find yourself using maybe 3 or 4 strategies at most. It all depends on your personality and and which ones appeal to you. However they are all included in the book because they all work, and as you get more experienced with understanding how markets work, what affects price movements, and you are more able to spot in play opportunities, you will find them all useful in the different market situations.

I've also covered the use of 'insurance' to cover for your trade and to lessen the loss should things turn against you, together with strategies and a description of how to recover from a losing trade and whether or not you should even attempt to recover a loss.

I'll also cover 'Scalping'. A technique that is often used in pre-race horseracing markets, but can also be used successfully on football matches.

I'm also including the very same statistic sites, (all free) that I use to source my selections, whether I'm looking for a First Half selection, an over/under goals candidate, a second half opportunity, a home win/LTD contender or even a strong away win choice.

With the huge amount of past performance data available online, which we will use to find our potential trades, we need to be highly selective and whittle down our selections to those that will give us the highest probability of success, so that when we have our selections made, we can be confident about adding them to our shortlist.

Free stat sites and free software, all of which I list, and in part
explain, will greatly help you find selections easily and quickly. A trader needs to spend as long as it takes each day to find their potential trades. This time is never wasted and without doing this research, I won't consider entering a trade.
The stats that we all use are the same. The only difference between traders is the interpretation of them and this is how the markets are formed. Your success depends in large part on your own interpretation being a good one, so do not skimp on this time. You can always use another persons selections as a basis for your research, but always make sure you double check what is suggested. This will also take out the option of just blaming someone else for your failure if the trade doesn't go to plan.

There is another huge factor in our decision to enter a trade and I'll explain later what this is and what it is you need to look out for and be aware of. By not taking this very important step into account, your chances of success are greatly diminished.

There are 19 Betfair Football markets to trade on from Match
Odds, Overs/Unders, Correct Scores Full and

Half Time. We have
strategies that cover most of them in one way or another.
The great thing about trading football on Betfair is that there are
matches being played in lots of different countries 365 days a year. There are always opportunities to profit.

This book is about making profits, but is also just as much as about NOT losing
money. There are some trades I wouldn't touch with someone else's
barge pole and they'll become more obvious to you as your work through the book.
And let none of us forget about the awesome power of compounding our profits, which is also covered in this book. I'll give you the solid reasons why you must compound for long term steady growth.
I'll also explain why you should never rely on someone elses judgement and go into a trade practically blind, and why you should never trade or consider trading just on a hunch, a whim, because you're bored, or just for something to do.

This book is all about learning to be smarter than the average
Betfair trader. Knowing how and when an

opportunity presents itself, and when to get involved and when not to get involved.
Remember there are plenty of traders out there waiting to take your money. Stop making it easy for them to run away with your cash. Over trading and over staking can lead to losses that are very uncomfortable. Remember that losing less is more important than winning. I'll help you with ways to make sure that losses are as small as can be.

Treat this book not as a purchase but as an investment in your
trading education. Use the information within and you can recover your investment many times over. There are no guarantees with trading of course. Its a totally individual pursuit, but I am secure in the knowledge that if you use the information I present wisely, you stand a much better chance of success than the traders that don't.

If you already have some trading experience, but you aren't doing particularly well and losing more than you should, then the first section of the book will most likely help you to uncover the reasons, and to get better results.
Traders don't have any excuses available for why they lose.

We can blame luck if we like, but at the final reckoning, it all comes down to us personally. If we lose too much of our bank, Don't make enough profit when it goes our way, or whatever scenario we think of, the buck stops with us. Never dwell on a poor outcome. Each trade is a completely new event and carrying over thoughts from a previous trade will only make it more difficult to think and act in line with our strategy.

If you want something you have never had before, you'll have to do things that you have never done before. Do nothing and nothing will change for you.

Treat trading as a business. Betfair commission are your expenses and your winnings are your profits and are tax free.

To be a successful trader you need to take action, don't buy this book read it and then forget about it. Use it and read it every day until all it contains becomes second nature to you. Highlight and make notes of sections that you deem to be most relevant. There is no waffle or padding. Absorb the info and become a better trader.

Welcome to the world of Trading Football On Betfair. In this book you will find information that I have collated from many many sources over the years.

It is regularly updated to keep abreast of changes and development's that I discover. Successful traders are always one step ahead of the opposition, i.e. the traders on the other side of the markets. So that's what you need to do.

Many people reading this book will have made the progression to trading via matched betting. If you haven't, I would urge you to give that a try first. You can make yourself some good money before the bookies realise what you are doing and you can use this money as your starting trading bank. That's what I did and it's a very safe way to profit quickly. I used a service called Bookie Busters by Mike Cruickshank, but there are other services. You've probably seen comments such as "I'm gubbed by so many bookies, I'm going to give trading a try". That's a natural thing to think when the bookies start to clamp down and don't allow you to get bets of reasonable size on, but let's be clear before we move on, football trading is not the Holy Grail most people think it is. There's a lot to learn and understand. It takes time and cannot be rushed into blindly. Just 'giving it a try' is not good enough. Do that and you will fail.

There is a huge difference between normal betting and trading. There is a lot of information to remember, as well as different techniques to get used to. Everything you're about to read is so very important to you and help you become a successful trader.

So many people fail to make it a success and it's generally for one of these reasons. Because they failed to take in the information, they lacked discipline, were impatient, or didn't pay enough attention to bank management. In other words they didn't stick to the rules and guidelines, or didn't heed the other advice within.

Don't include yourself in the majority who fail. Stay positive as much as you can. Learn to trust your own judgement and just as importantly, trust in those who are already successful and have trodden the same path. You can learn a lot from the right people. They've all made mistakes, and have all learned some harsh lessons. You too will have experiences in your trading career that make you question your decision to trade. I hope to help you avoid the worst ones and if you can find other traders that you trust, and listen to them too, you will have a much greater chance of surviving in the football markets.

I source my selections from many free stat sites. I check and double check them, and only when I'm satisfied that the selection's I have found are of the highest possible calibre, and have the greatest probability of the outcome I have forecast, will I invest my money and trade on them.

I not only look for reasons to make a match a selection, I also look for reasons NOT to make it a selection. I would suggest you do the same. Seek out any 'red flags'. If team news causes you concern, such as internationals taking place, if any key players are injured, if there is a management change, all these along with lots of other variables need taking into account.

So, take your time, understand the rules as I have laid them out, stick within your own personal liabilities and bank, adhere to the guidelines of each strategy, do not enter a trade unless you know when you will exit, be it for a profit or a loss. And most of all... be patient.

Patience is your greatest weapon. Successful trading can be broken down to the fact that patient traders make the most money from impatient ones.

Always wait for the right opportunity to enter the trade you've chosen. Do not allow yourself to be put under stress or pressure at any time, it is not worth it. Allowing that to happen will affect the way you trade and ultimately your success.

Sometimes goals will happen when we want them, sometimes they won't happen and sometimes they will happen at the wrong time for us. It's just like the prices movements, we have no control over them. What we do have control over is how we react to those events. This is where personal judgement, experience and patience comes in. No matter what the matches in play events are, we will have a strategy in place to adapt our position in response to them.

We cannot win every trade. That's impossible.

There are simply too many outside factors that can affect us when we trade, but we can be ready to adapt. You will hear a lot of talk about having a plan and sticking to it. That is a lot harder to implement during a match than it is before kick off. This is because we will have formed opinions about how the match is being played, or which team is having the most of the possession etc. It can pay to remember that these are only your personal opinions. Other people will have the opposite opinion. That is how a market is actually formed, so be ready. Have a strategy in place and do not hesitate to implement it when the stats tell you it's time to.

This will put you ahead of a lot of traders, especially the countless number who are planless and trade with their heart.

Be a patient of the patient traders that take money from the impatient ones. Then do it, day in and day out.

Learn one or two strategies at a time. Practice with them using small stakes and when your happy that you can use them without having to think about what to do next, learn another strategy. Rinse and repeat until eventually using the strategies becomes second nature.

Look at learning to trade successfully as a

marathon and not a sprint. Trying to force trades to get in on the action never ends well.

Conquer your fear of missing out at the beginning and your future trades will be better for not having that to contend with.

Bank Management.

The number one thing that you need to understand, right from the outset is good bank management. Without it, you aren't doomed to failure, but your progress will be severely hindered.

Have a bank that you are totally detached from. Look at it as already gone. That isn't to say you don't guard it with your life, as you do. It is the most important thing to you. You won't be able to trade without it, so never take unnecessary risks with it. It's your life blood.

Never risk too big of a percentage of your bank on any trade. My strategy is to never risk more than 3% of my bank on any one trade, and that will only ever be on trades that I think are the most secure. The majority of the time I will risk 1%. This ensures that I can stay in the markets for the long haul, even if I do have some very bad lapses of judgement. We need to always be in control of what is happening to our capital.

Liability.

Stay within your maximum liability at all times whether backing or laying. So if your liability is £10, this amount is the maximum you will use to place a back bet. If you're laying, £10 is still your maximum, so in other words you could lay £10 at 2.0, or £5 at 3, or £2.50 at 5. Each of these bets has a liability of £10. Trading software will help you to determine what your stake will be when laying at other less obvious odds.

Have a plan and stick to it.
After your meticulous research, the selections you made are your starting point. Combine them with a chosen strategy, which you will arrive at after studying the stats of the match, and then stick to your plan. Know when you will enter and exit your trade and make sure you do not deviate from it. As you become more experienced in the markets, you could possibly take a few more chances with your entry and exit points. You'll have developed a feel for certain markets over time and after watching hundreds of them, but when starting out, stick to the plan.

Each strategy has its own unique entry/exit points to guide you, but they are not set in stone, and as you gain more experience, your entry and exit points will become more flexible.

When it comes to statistics and information about a football match, I think it's wise to err on the side of too much rather than too little. Seek out all the info that you can. This will give you a lead on people that trade on instinct or fancy. Follow clubs and players on twitter and other social media.

Take into account team news. Is the top scorer/key player out injured or rested? Has the manager been sacked/changed? Is the weather likely to have any bearing on the game?

Perhaps the most important reason for siding with a team, I find is, is there a reason that they need to win? Is it a vital promotion or relegation game? Is there a more important game ahead in the next few days? All of these things are taken into account by the savvy trader. Don't overlook them.

It's a comforting feeling going into a trade with everything covered and knowing you're on the right side from the start. You are developing an edge..

Having chosen a selection, a trader has to know when to enter and when they are going to exit, for a profit or controlled loss. Follow the advice in the strategies ahead for entry points and when you have decided to exit, make sure you do so when the market has settled and your profit or loss is acceptable to you. If you wait longer than you intended, your profit can evaporate or your losses grow.

Remember that when you do that you are gambling. It is a more subtle form admittedly, but a gamble nonetheless.

Be patient. Do not rush into a market with little thought. There will always be plenty of opportunities and you should always choose your entry time to get the best value from your trade, regardless of whether you backed first or laid.

Taking a Loss.

Sometimes things do not go to plan and you will need to do something to lessen your potential loss.

Don't just sit there doing nothing and hoping. There's no point in having your bank bleed away. Stick a plaster on it and it will stop the bleeding. Once you have done that you cannot lose any more money and you're protecting your bank.

Taking a loss should be as simple as taking profit, but this isn't usually the case. I found it one of the biggest hurdles to becoming profitable. I would ignore my exit point, in the hope that the game would turn around, and I would be able to trade out for less of a loss, or maybe even profit. Don't be like I was, don't even begin to think like that. It will save you a lot of angst in the long run.

If you felt it was a good trade, but it did not go the way you wanted and you STOPPED the bleed when it was small, you did the right thing.

Start to really believe that getting out with a small loss, or getting out with a small profit has exactly the same effect on your psyche.

So what if you traded out for a loss only to see a last minute goal go in. You made your decision and acted on it in line with your plan and did the right thing. That's all there is to it. Move on to the next trade. There is no point dwelling on what might have been. Spend your time more productively on figuring out your next selection and plan.

It's all part of your education. Get used to taking a losing trade on the chin, to feeling no emotional pain and enter the next trade without that loss affecting your next decision in any way. That is your goal. It might not come easily to start with, but you'll get better at it with practice.

Take your profit at every opportunity.

Whenever the match goes in your favour take your profit and get out!

Hedge across all other outcomes. Do not be greedy and hope for more, as you may well wish you hadn't. A lot of times with this strategy, you will feel more pain and its much better to lessen the chances of that at every opportunity.

If you don't use trading software, and it's not important when starting out, use Betfair's 'Cash Out' option. It's a quick and easy one click procedure. On occasion, it may cost you a tiny percentage of your profit, but in the long run the speed of exit makes it worthwhile.

Whilst trading software doesn't make you a better trader, it can help improve your efficiency. You'll be able to access market information easier and place orders faster than you would be able to without any software. More information on that is to follow.

One-click betting allows you to preset a stake amount and place a
bet with one click of the mouse. It cuts down on clicks and improves your trading efficiency. When using the Betfair website to trade, you have to click on the odds, enter a stake amount and click again to confirm your bet. It doesn't sound like much, but you can miss out on profitable trading opportunities if you're
too slow entering the market.

Another big advantage of using trading software is that it allows you to use stake amounts below Betfair's £2 minimum.

Placing dutch trades is also much easier. Dutching is just betting on multiple outcomes on the same event to produce a profit no matter what.
Trading software can make this much easier, by calculating stake amounts, allowing you bet almost automatically. It also gives you the ability to set stop losses.

The betfair market web site also has a simple to use dutching facility.

Here's how to use it. Using the scoreline 2-1 and 1-2 as an example,

open up the correct score market and click on 2-1 and 1-2 as if you were about to back them.
Next click on the stake button and enter your bet amount into the box and press confirm. You will then see that Betfair has done the calculation covering both scores with the appropriate stakes for the dutch bet.
Look at the correct scores and you will see how much profit you will have if either of your choices are correct.
If you're happy with the amounts, click confirm on the bet slip and the trade will be placed. It's as simple as that.

Software is a matter of personal choice and my advice is to try out
each one to find out which suits you best. They are all have slightly different lay outs and options. So test them all and see which suits your trading style.
All trading software providers give you a free trial so you can get to know the
programme before purchase.
Having tried several my own preference is Bet Trader from Racing Traders. the layout suits me and the after sales support is excellent. In addition its web based and works on W10 or Mac.

* * *

Bet Angel from Peter Webb is another very good software
programme and it is feature packed.

A Geeks Toy used solely by Caan Berry in his trading is another
well known and very good programme. Others such as Fairbot and
Traderline I know nothing about so I cannot comment. Whatever
trading software you use will make your trading life easier, but it doesn't make any decisions. That's down to you.

https://racingtraders.co.uk/bettrader/

https://www.betangel.com

http://www.geekstoy.com/en/download

Moving on..

Stick to the advice given for each strategy. Do not deviate in any way or you will find yourself in trouble, so enter and exit every trade when the strategy tells you to do so.

In addition to the above, here are some more thoughts and ideas I would recommend to everyone, especially those who are new or fairly new to trading. For the more experienced traders, it may help you to understand what has been holding you back and why you're losing more money than you should be.

To start, set up a £200 trading bank and only use 1% of it as a maximum risk until you're comfortable with what you're doing. Even now I rarely go above 1% and if I do, 3% is the absolute maximum liability.

Never enter a trade until you're happy with the entry point and always know when your going to exit for a profit or a controlled loss. I know I keep repeating myself, but I do it with purpose. It's the best way to make this information stick.

Do not trade on a whim or follow someone else's trade unless you're happy that the selection is a good one, based on your own analysis of the stats. You must always know the risk involved and you must always stay within your set liability whether backing or laying.

How do you know if the suggestion has been well researched or if it has been made on a whim? You don't, unless you check for yourself. Are the in play stats of the suggested trade accurate and are they good enough to warrant the investment? Make your own mind up.

Make sure you really understand the above and what it means to your ultimate success. Stick solidly to the guidelines and do not vary from them. Keep records of every trade you make and use this accumulated knowledge to improve your analysis.

Seek out the ways and means to find your own selections. It is never good to rely on anyone else, especially when it comes to trading. The interpretation of statistics is a purely personal thing, so do it yourself, strive to improve and become self sufficient.

You can always join social media groups and talk to other people about trading and match stats. A quick google will throw up a plethora of such groups. But like the stats themselves, how you interpret what you see is up to you. Make up your own mind about whether they are a benefit or hindrance to your progress.

Do not try to emulate others too closely. Always remember that the screenshots of winning trades and huge profits that are a common sight on twitter, can be easily created in Photoshop, so tread carefully. Be yourself and set your own goals. Like any other skill, with practice, trading will become second nature to you. Learn it the right way from the beginning and you will be set up for a lifetime.

Your strategies and methodically researched selections, and how much risk you are prepared to take and for what reward are all personal. When combined, they help form your edge. Always protect your bank, work smarter, don't over trade, and sit some games out if you are in any doubt about your interpretation of the stats, and you will enjoy your trading more.

It is important not to be swayed too much by any emotion, and not to let any that do crop up interfere with your judgement. Always base your decisions on the facts as presented by the stats that you're assessing. For example, if you've made a selection as a probable trade and you suddenly think to yourself, "this team are 18th in the league, they will never score when they are playing away to the league leader," but you've previously noticed that this 18th position team has scored an away goal against the top 5 sides in the league this season, you are making an emotional judgement based on something other than the evidence of the stats. Emotions can be very strong and can alter your perception. Always be aware of them.

It could be that the team you support are playing and you have an emotional interest in the result. This can sway your judgement and stop you looking for statistical evidence of whats likely to happen in the match, in a non judgemental and analytical way.

Trust the stats and don't allow emotions to hinder you.

I'm a trader not a gambler, is a good motto to adopt

And don't just take my word for it. The well

known trader Psychoff on Twitter said in an interview, "we need stats to give us the likelihood of an outcome".

Always be aware of whats happening in a match that has kicked off. If its not going as your reading of the stats suggested it would, consider getting out of the trade as soon as you can. Your bank will suffer if you dither.

If traders treated £5 like it was £50 or £10 like it was £100 how many would lay above 2.0? How many would back at a price below 1.40?

I know that people with a background as an ordinary punter are more likely to baulk at these prices, but winning traders are comfortable in these areas. So get comfortable too. Successful traders only ever need a few ticks of movement to make profits. It's simply a matter of taking those ticks over and over again.

I don't win every time, but I do expect to profit over the long term or I wouldn't consider doing this in the first place. The other night for example my lay bet was queued in at 1.10 on the Napoli game, the price dropped to 1.18 or thereabouts when the goal went in on 90', and my lay was cancelled. I didn't win but I also didn't lose, so there is no point in stressing over what may have happened if my lay bet had been put in at 1.2 instead. All this will do is unsettle your thinking and that is all that separates the patient traders from the impatient.

Treat a 'scratch' trade as a winning trade. You tried, you entered and exited the trade, but you didn't win. You didn't lose though either.

Treat trading like a business. Expect lossses, but also expect to profit more. Short term dips can be looked on as a business expense. After all, your profits are tax free so it's a good business to be in and that is a great incentive to want to get better at it.

And how often have I seen it mentioned... I would have done it but the price was rubbish.. An early goal scuppered my trade... So what. You've lost nothing

Move on to your next selection and if the price offered is too low for you, move up a market. For example from O1.5 goals to O2.5, or from O2.5 to O3.5.

And yes you can fully or partly recover a losing trade but ask yourself is it worth the extra risk?

Sometimes I do this, but most of the time I don't. I've learned to accept small losses knowing that in the long run I'll soon make it back.

Go above your liability whether backing or laying

and you're not just asking for trouble, you're standing in the line of fire and putting yourself under stress and pressure for no reason. Like them or not these are the facts. I have discovered them the hard way and now my whole trading regimen is based around them.

Methodical Research:

I do not believe there is a trade anyone should ever consider getting involved in without doing research on the event beforehand. Doing so is complete foolishness and your bank will eventually will pay the price.

This may sound obvious but think about how often you may have been tempted to trade in play and get your first bet in as quickly as possible, so as not to miss the supposed good current price. Don't let the fear of missing out interrupt your method. There are always plenty of markets to get involved in and no matter how good a trade looks, if you haven't done the research and you are basing your trade on a fancy, you are going to lose in the long run. Of course there will be times when you get it right and make a large profit, but don't let that little ego stroke fool you. To be a long term successful trader you need a plan and you need to stick to it like a limpit.

Spend some time each morning looking at the days upcoming events. Make some notes as I do. You are trying to give yourself an advantage over other traders. That is all you need to do. Stay a step in front of the majority. Never ever trade blind. You need as much information about the teams and their stats as possible before even considering starting a trading position.

After kick off, if you spot an opportunity to trade in play, do more research there and then before getting involved. With the high speed internet that we are now all used to, it only takes a couple of minutes to check multiple sources to cross check the stats, with what our reading of the match is telling us. Check not only the in play stats, but find out if the teams usually score early or late in their games, look also at recent past performances for both teams home and away. You will get quicker at doing this with practice and so you'll get better at mopping up the value.

You need to be spending as much time as you can afford on your research. Most people cannot be bothered and give the stats a cursory glance before deciding to open a trade. This is pretty much gambling and is highly unlikely to be profitable in the long run.

Do your research, be methodical, make your selections, set up your trading plan and stick to it. Do not be tempted into other trades that you haven't fully researched. There be dragons.

Using stats software helps cut your research time, but you must still check other sources once your selections are narrowed down. Keep your eyes on what is happening before the match. Follow your team on twitter, open up the sports websites, do all you can to be as informed as you can. It is eye opening to see how many bad trades can be avoided by assessing a team sheet, or by watching a match and deciding if there is any intent to score in the teams that are playing.

If you combine pre-match and in-play analysis, as the wise traders do, your trades will be at least twice as strong in my opinion. You are now armed with two sets of serious information

If you discover a trading opportunity, forensically examine it before putting your money at risk. Try to find reasons not to open a position. Scour your internet sources. If you have done this and you have found no reasons to avoid it, it may well be a trade worth starting.

Don't lie to yourself. This is the worst thing you can do. Some people like to go on social media and tell others about how well they have done with their days trading, but rather than saying how many points they have made, they talk in pounds.

People that are selling tips, or promising untold riches for very little effort use this ploy all the time.

The figures need context.

This willy waving/ virtue signalling might impress some people and even make the trader themselves feel better, but a days profit of £1200 makes no sense without the staking being taken into account. This is something that the beginning trader needs to be aware of. Don't be fooled by peoples bragging. £1200 profit might be brilliant but it might also be terrible. Never be impressed by figures without context.

In Play Stats:

We can find in play stats everywhere. Betfair, Bet 365, Flash Score, Live scores, Sofa Scores, all provide stats that we can access before trading. What they all have in common is they're usually all different and rarely use the same sources for the information.

One site may register a shot on target from outside the box that went straight into the goal keeper's hands, whilst another site may just take it as a shot not on target. Some register corners quickly while others do not. Shots on target inside the box are far better than shots from outside the box.

So what good is a mish-mash of stats that may or may not be reliable?

Well just be aware of these shortcomings. They are a very rough guide at best. If you have access to a live feed or can watch on the TV, that is much the best way.

Discipline:

This is what separates the good traders from the not so good. As we are all aware strong discipline is the bedrock of every good trader and you should aim to build solidly on that foundation.

If your potential selection doesn't fill you with the utmost confidence, have the discipline to leave it alone and not trade on it. This kind of discipline is often overlooked. It is easy to talk yourself into opening a trade on a match that you are not entirely convinced is going to go your way. There is a nagging doubt, but your ego over rides that doubt, because the need for some action in the markets is stronger than your discipline to abandon it. Remember that a no bet is much better than a losing one.

Look forward in your mind and visualise how you might feel if you did enter the market and it went against you. This kind of visualisation is just as useful as looking ahead and visualising yourself winning, if not more so.

Don't dwell on trades that go against you. Sending offs, penalties, injuries to key players all happen. They cannot be reliably foreseen so don't waste mental energy on them. Move on to the next trade.

 Don't let a good winning trade make you think

that you are God's gift to trading. Also don't let getting it wrong make you think that you know nothing and should give up trying. You are somewhere on a constant line between those two extremes and the longer you spend slap bang in the middle of them, the better a trader you will become.

Variance? Now there is a concept that has been used as an excuse by many for a long, long time. It's easy to blame variance for a loss. If you have had a good run of successful trades and have now hit a few that were not so good, then you could say it was variance kicking in. Don't say that, as it's no such thing. Stop using that word to justify a trade you should not have entered in the first place.

Here is a simplified version of what variance actually is. There are more in depth explanations online, for people that are interested.

Variance applies to things that have a known outcome, such as slots. These infernal machines have a percentage for the owner of them built into the design. Over time that built in percentage will seem to fluctuate for anyone who doesn't have the intelligence to realise that it is mathematically impossible for them to win on them. If a machine pays out a lot of jackpots, variance will ensure that the owners profit margin stays the same by providing a run of losing spins. There is no other way it can do it.

With a sports match or a horse race or any other event whose outcome is not certain and on which the odds of a certain conclusion can fluctuate, both before and during the event, then variance cannot apply. For it to work out over time there has to be a known conclusion and percentage chance of this conclusion for it to apply to.

So stop saying that variance has bitten you on the bum. It's an excuse that you need to stop using. When you have simply entered a position that you shouldn't have or delayed getting out of one to cut your losses, it was nobodies fault but your own.

Have the discipline to take a break. Have at least 1-2 days off a week. Make sure you take enough exercise. Sitting at a computer for hours is not good for your health. Trading is something that you need to enjoy to do well. If you ignore your health to do it, your body will remind you that you can't ignore it, by giving you an ache or an illnesss to force you to stop. Don't let it get to that point. Discipline yourself to prevent it.

Don't be insular. Talk to your partner or friends about your trading. I'm old enough to remember British Telecom and their advertising slogan " Its

Good To Talk," and agree with it. If you have a bad day share it with someone, the same if you have had a cracking day. Trading can be emotionally charged and keeping it inside and only talking to yourself about it is not the best policy. I have stressed that it is important for you to remind yourself often to keep your stress levels under control, by not having too large a liability, or letting trades run for too long. This is the best thing to do, but it doesn't always happen. So accept that in these instances it is good to talk.

Trading should be fun as well as profitable, so strive to keep it that way.

Selecting your potential trades and statistic sites.

Selecting good matches which will allow you to trade well and consistently is your most important job. It's not the easiest thing to do when you first start out, but with practice it gets easier.

The sites I have listed below are the ones that I use, and they work for me and suit my style and time for study. Of course you may find others that you prefer, so feel free to experiment. Nothing about trading is set in stone so make sure you try out as many different sources as you can.

If for example you're looking for matches which have a high probability of a First Half Goal in order to trade the FHG market, then you will be looking for sides who have scored in the first 45 minutes of their previous matches at least 80% of the time. That includes both the Home and Away side. So you will be looking at both sides last 10 games H/A and you will be looking for a First Half Goal in 8 out of 10 of their most recent games.

Use this software site to find the matches that meet that criteria. It's free, it's easy to use and it's fast. All you need do is ask it to find games that match your settings.

http://soccerstatstracker.com/english/download.htm/

Always remember to update each time you use this site.

The same site will also help you quickly find, and after a few seconds of searching, present you with a list showing the likelihood of the match having O1.5, O2.5, O3.5 goals. There are all kinds of other stats in the software, but while you get used to it I would suggest sticking to the goals markets.

I'll list below the overall percentage I'm looking for in the different markets when using these stat sites to cover the different strategies. By 'overall' I mean the joint percentage of both sides in the match.

From the list I get I then dig deeper to see if they've got those results playing sides of equal quality.

First Half Goal 80%

BTS (BTTS) 65%

O1.5 Goals 90%

O2.5 Goals 70%

O3.5 Goals 50%

While there are of course teams that score most goals in the first half, the majority of teams score in the second half which is the reason why the second half stats show the second forty-five produces more goals than the first, also both sides know they have to score in the second half if they are to win. In the first half there isn't as much urgency generally.

Goal times, when goals are scored and conceded are also an important factor. Another way of looking at the stats is if both sides have a low (below 20%) 0-0 HT score rate it is a good indicator for a FHG.

You will often find that the top 5 sides in the league concede less goals (that's why they're in the top 5) and their matches are less likely to end in a draw. That's another good reason to lay the draw.

Another good indicator is to look for sides that have a good record of scoring more than 2 goals at home. Also be on the look out for teams lower down the league that have a good away scoring record, especially their last five or six games. The more recent the statistics the better. Sometimes the free scoring home teams, can also be free conceding, so look out for those. The two playing each other are usually solid goals matches.

However, take nothing for granted. No matter how good the pre-match stats are, what happens on the day is what really matters. As we all know, once a match kicks off anything can happen.

I don't get involved in a game that has had a red card. If a red card is given after I have opened my trade, I immediately look to exit as soon as possible. Most of the time this can be for scratch or a small loss. Don't hesitate when these situations arise. The trade has become highly volatile and you are best exiting and moving on.

If a match is in play and I spot an opportunity, I always make sure, as far as possible, that both sides are trying to score, or failing that, one side is totally dominating the other. If I don't see either, I stay well away.

As I focus on the goals market, and whether it's an LTD1/LTD2, Full Match LTD, O1.5/O2.5, BTS. I want both sides to be trying their best for me. If there is nothing at stake, then it's less likely that the teams will be going for it and that is not what I want. I'm always looking for all 22 players on the pitch to be playing to win. These matches are manna from heaven.

Another sometimes lucrative area to concentrate on is from around the 80 minute onwards mark in matches. It can be quite cheap to lay the current score at this point, and if both teams are eager for the win, you can be in a low liability, large profit situation quite quickly.

My go to site for all things statistical is https://www.adamchoi.co.uk/

Here you will find all the stats you could ever need including FHG's, Overs, BTS, Corners and more. It's simple to use, effective and it's also kept up to date.

Here's a very good site for comparing at a glance how teams have performed against other teams over their last 5/6 games.

http://www.soccerstats.com

Yet another very good site and this site also has a mobile app for those on the move and it's one I use a lot for up to date in play stats.

https://www.sofascore.com

Below are some sites I use less often. Each has its own particular use to me when I'm doing my research, so take a look and see if you find them useful.

http://www.thestatsdontlie.com/football/stats/

https://uk.soccerway.com

http://www.kickoffprofits.com/free-stats/

https://www.over25tips.com/free-football-betting-tips/

And of course the ever popular

https://www.flashscores.co.uk

So now we can move onto the strategies. As I've mentioned before, learn each strategy fully before moving onto the next. Always start off with low stakes until you're comfortable with the procedure. There's plenty of time and plenty of year round opportunities.

The entry and exit points are as important as each other and I strongly urge you to adhere to them until such time you have the experience to be more flexible. As trader's we seek to profit at every opportunity and again I urge you to take your profit as soon as you can. It is far better to take 40-60% consistently than losing it and taking 0% by over staying in a trade that went the wrong way. Many times sides have equalised soon after going a goal down and you're suddenly looking at a red screen when you could have easily got out with a profit.

Greed is one of the worst possible emotions to have, gamblers know it only too well. It doesn't pay and it never will.

And bear in mind also that instead of going in with your full stake up to your set liability, consider staking 20-25% at a time (Backing or Laying), that way by drip feeding your stake into the market your taking a huge advantage on the price increase or decrease and that means more profit when it goes your way.

Before you get involved with any trade always ensure that there's plenty of money in the market, a lack of 'liquidity' could well mean that when the time comes to exit your trade you may find you cannot.

Again this is so very important and must be watched carefully.

On occasion, some games that Betfair lists as going in play do not. If you put your stakes in before kick off on these matches, you're stuck with it and you'll not be able to trade out or exit. Annoying when it happens but thankfully it doesn't happen often.

As you can see, each strategy has a code name. This is to make it easier for you to recognise each trading strategy and in doing so makes them easier to remember until they become second nature to you.

Here are my selection results for Saturday and Sunday 28th/29th April 2018 these are the result of methodical research which anyone can achieve with practice and perseverance. As I mentioned earlier, time spent researching is time well spent. Don't be lazy and try to short cut. It will cost you in the long run.

Every selection listed was posted many hours ahead of kick off and the results posted below are the full time score. The figures in brackets are the current league positions.

Saturday 28th April.

O2.5 Goals
14:30 Won Bayern München (1) vs. Eintracht Frankfurt (7)
15:00 Won Crystal Palace (14) vs. Leicester City (9)
18:00 Won Atlanta United (3) vs. Montreal Impact (18)
18:45 Scratch Won Almere City (10) vs. Volendam (11)
18:45 1-0 Fortuna Sittard (2) vs. PSV II (5)
18:45 Won AZ II (15) vs. De Graafschap (4)

LTD (Full Match)
12:30 0-0 Liverpool (3) Stoke City (19)
14:30 Won Bayern München (1) Eintracht Frankfurt (7)
15:00 0-0 Wolverhampton Wanderers (1) Sheffield Wednesday (15)
18:00 Won Young Boys (1) v Luzern (3)

O1.5 Goals W10
10:50 Won Sydney (1) vs Melbourne Victory (4)
14:00 Won Clermont (4) vs Nîmes (2)
15:00 Won Crystal Palace (14) vs. Leicester City (9)
15:00 Won Austria Wien (6) vs. Mattersburg (7)

16:00 Won Olympique Lyonnais (3) vs Nantes (9)
14:30 Won Bayern München (1) vs. Eintracht Frankfurt (7)
18:00 Won Young Boys (1) vs Luzern (3)
18:00 0-1 Lausanne Sport (10) vs Grasshopper (7)
18:00 Won Atlanta United (3) vs. Montreal Impact (18)
18:45 Won Almere City (10) vs. Volendam (11)
18:45 1-0 Fortuna Sittard (2) vs. PSV II (5)
18:45 Won AZ II (15) vs. De Graafschap (4)

BTS YES
18:45 2-0 Almere City (10) vs. Volendam (11)
18:45 Won AZ II (15) vs. De Graafschap (4)

FHG LTD1/W1
10:50 Won Sydney (1) vs Melbourne Victory (4)
14:00 0-0 recovered Scratch Clermont (4) vs Nîmes (2)
14:30 Won Bayern München (1) vs Eintracht Frankfurt (7)
14:30 Won Schalke 04 (2) vs Borussia M'gladbach (8)
15:15 Won Real Sociedad (11) vs Athletic Club (14)
18:00 0-0 recovered Scratch Young Boys (1) vs Luzern (3)
18:00 0-0 Lost Lausanne Sport (10) vs

Grasshopper (7)
18:00 Won Atlanta United (3) vs. Montreal Impact (18)
18:45 0-0 recovered Scratch Ajax II (1) vs MVV (9)

Home Win
14:30 Bayern Munich Won
15:00 Wolves 0-0 Lost
15:00 Kettering Won
16:00 Lyon Won
17:00 Roma Won
18:00 Young Boys Won
19:00 Monaco 0-0 Lost
19:15 Plzen Won

Sunday 29th April

O2.5 Goals
13:30 Won ADO Den Haag (9) vs PSV (1)
13:30 Won Heracles (11) vs Utrecht (5)
15:00 Won Rapperswil-Jona (5) vs Wohlen (10)
16:20 Won Al Ain (1) vs Al Dhafra (10)
17:00 Won Brøndby (1) vs Nordsjælland (3)
19:45 0-1 Torino (10) vs Lazio (3)

W3.5
15:00 Won Rapperswil-Jona (5) vs Wohlen (10)
17:00 Won Brøndby (1) vs Nordsjælland (3)

* * *

LTD (Full Match)
20:00 Won PSG (1) v Guingamp (10)

O1.5 Goals W10
13:30 Won ADO Den Haag (9) vs PSV (1)
13:30 Won Groningen (12) vs Excelsior (10)
13:30 Won Ajax (2) vs AZ (3)
13:30 Won Heracles (11) vs Utrecht (5)
14:15 Won West Ham United (15) vs Manchester City (1)
15:00 Won Rapperswil-Jona (5) vs Wohlen (10)
16:00 Won Angers SCO (14) vs Olympique Marseille (4)
16:20 Won Al Ain (1) vs Al Dhafra (10)
17:00 Won Brøndby (1) vs Nordsjælland (3)
17:00 Won Galatasaray (1) vs Besiktas (2)
19:45 0-1 Torino (10) vs Lazio (3)

FHG LTD1/W1
13:30 Won Groningen (12) vs Excelsior (10)
13:30 0-0 Zwolle (8) vs Willem II (14)
13:30 Won ADO Den Haag (9) vs PSV (1)
14:15 Won West Ham United (15) vs. Manchester City (1)
15:00 Won Rapperswil-Jona (5) vs Wohlen (10)
17:00 Won Galatasaray (1) vs Besiktas (2)
19:45 0-0 Torino (10) vs Lazio (3)
20:00 Won PSG (1) vs Guingamp (10)

Trading Strategies

Note that 1 Point equals your liability whether Backing or Laying.

First Half Strategies.

W1
With this strategy we are looking for a game that will be 1-0 or 0-1 at half-time. I have called this my W1 Strategy, but it could also be called LTD1, (Lay The Draw 1) or FHG (First Half Goal.) The name might change but our target is the same, just one goal in the first half.
The one score you don't want is 0-0, so the aim will be to avoid those as much as possible. The average game has one goal in the first half and that is what we are trying to take advantage of. Careful selections, ie. those with above 80% overall from past results will give you the highest probability of the outcome you're after.

Trading W1
We are only going to be in this trade for 20 minutes or so. At half time we are out of it, hopefully with a profit.
All we do is watch the in-play price of the 0-0 scoreline. When it hits 2.50 we lay it for 1Pt. This will normally happen around 25 minute mark.

Don't go beyond that. If there is a goal before you get matched then forget it, it's is a no-trade. It happens and there's nothing we can do about that.

The average number of first half goals is 1.1 so it is highly likely that a game will be 1-0 or 0-1 at half-time. Furthermore with this system, any number of goals after the first one means a win for us.

So all you need to do is lay the Half Time 0-0 score for 1Pt at 2.50 or below. You may not be comfortable laying at the price I do, so just wait for a little longer until the price is more to your liking.

If you don't like to miss out on a match that the stats and your eyes tell you is going to have a goal, you can open your trade by dripping the stake in. Lay half a point at 3.00 and then the other half point at 2.00. This gives you the same liability.

When the expected goal is scored, your trade is successful.

LTD1

This is again uses the half time market.

We will lay the draw at odds no greater than 2.20 for 0.5Pt only.

If there is a heavy favourite involved, usually the

home team, and goals are expected, the draw odds may be much higher, so you have two options.

Drip lay the draw up to 0.5pt liability or set your lay with 0.5pt liability no higher than 2.20 (make sure you select the Keep In Play button) and wait to see if you get matched.
Wait in play until the draw odds have reached 2.20. If a goal is scored before that happens its a no trade.
When your HT draw odds are matched, then Dutch 1-0/0-1 in the Half Time Correct score market for your remaining 0.5Pt.

That's all there is to it. When a goal goes in you can green the draw and the dutch trade, so you win twice. When there is a goal, always take your profit on both but of course let the market settle first.

Green up the draw first of all and when that's done, do the correct score market. We do it in that order because by doing so your taking profit off 2 markets. Just do not hang around waiting, get out with your profits... both of them!

Obviously the only half time score we don't want is 0-0 because you lose both your trades. These scorelines do happen though, but by selecting only the strongest matches using the stats, we will be successful much more than we would y simply placing a regular right or wrong bet.

If your LTD1 was unsuccessful and the HT score was 0-0 then consider using the W1o Trade (see Full match Strategies) to recover your losses. Of course if the 2nd half only produces 1 goal it will mean you've lost both trades. It's unlikely that will happen often enough to concern you, as long as you've chosen the right game to trade with all the right pre-match stats in place.

Tip: Select your trade with the proviso that BOTH sides have an O1.5 goals strike rate of around 80%, so that if needed you can easily recover your losing FHG trade.
So if LTD1 is 0-0 at HT use the **W1o** trade to recover your lost stake. You will find that at HT the O1.5 price is high enough to take advantage of with less of a liability, and you may even profit over all.
Every game selected for **W1o** (see the Tip mentioned above) will also have been assessed and high rated to give 2 goals in the game. More often than not you will get your 2 goals and your trade will be a scratch trade, so nothing gained and nothing lost.

***

2nd Half Strategies

LTD2 (2nd Half Lay The Draw)
This is where the HT score is level, 0-0/1-1 usually, so we're looking at the the Match Odds Market. This trade is not one you can select pre-match.
With LTD2 you will make your own call on whether to trade or not based purely upon your assessment of what has taken place in the first half.

If you're happy with the first half in play stats, there's been plenty of attempts on goal from BOTH sides, (8 shots on target between them,) and there are plenty of corners (6 Minimum) then you may wish to open a trading position. You should only Lay the Draw at odds of less than 3.0 never above. If this means waiting in play before you enter, do it. Never lay above 3.0 and the lower the odds the better.

The reason is, if the underdog scores the odds will barely move as the market will expect the favourites to equalise. Laying below 3.0 gives you a better chance of some profit but be aware that after the first goal the game will open up especially if the favourite is at home and losing.

* * *

When the goal goes in take your profit. If the favourite scores it will be higher than if the underdog scores, but still profit. The later in the game the goal is scored, the better and you must always take your green.

Also decide at what point you will exit the trade if no goals have been scored. You may decide that you'll get out no later than the 75 minute mark or when the price to back has dropped to half of the price that you laid the draw at. It will be a loss of course, but it won't be a full loss of your stake, like it would be for a normal punter. Always remember to protect your bank.

The good news is that the majority of football matches have most goals scored in the 2nd half, so you have a better chance of success.

Only 11% of matches end 0-0 at full time. You can if you wish trade out for scratch or a small loss around 65 minutes if you feel the game isn't going anywhere. Just be aware most goals are scored in the second half as I've mentioned, and it's in the second half games are usually won. LTD2 is a simple and very profitable strategy and one that anyone starting out should use.

* * *

WHTFAV (Half Time Favourite)

As in the example trade above, the match selected for this trade is not based on the pre-match stats, but because of the in play facts. You are looking for a specific scoreline at HT with a strong home favourite and with good intent shown from the stats from the first half.

It's a simple second half trade you may wish to consider when you come across a 0-0 HT score. Check the in play stats and if the home team is seen as dominating the game and they are also the favourite in the match odds markets then:

Back the Home team Favourite at odds above 2.50 for 0.5pt(stake) and Lay U1.5 goals for 0.5pt at around 1.50.

If the Home team scores to go 1-0, green up the home win. Leave the U1.5 in place. If it stays 1-0 at FT your profit will be around 50% and if the score goes 2-0/1-1 you make around 150%.

The risks is if the away side scores and the game ends 0-1. Of course if it ends 0-0 you lose 1pt. Similarly if the away side goes 0-1 up you lose 0.5Pt and if the home side levels to 1-1 you make scratch. With a FT win for the Home Favourite

2-1 or more, you again win both trades. The risk to reward is therefore quite acceptable in my opinion.

W2SH

With W2SH we are looking at games that may have several scoreline's at HT and where we expect the game to have at least 2 goals in the 2nd half. Use your strong o2.5 selections and also the in play stats from the 1st half to help make sure that you are only going in on the strongest contenders.

This is a strategy that you will enter at half-time. As we are all aware, most goals are scored in the 2nd half of matches (47%) and so we have a very good chance of success.

You will set up your trade based upon the following HT scores and set your target Scores as below:

If the score is:

0-0* your target scores are 1-1/2-0 or 0-2/1-1

0-1 your target scores are 0-3/1-2

* * *

1-0 your target scores are 2-1/3-0

1-1* your target scores are 2-2/3-1 or 1-3/2-2

*We would always look toward the favourite if the score is 0-0 or 1-1.
In a tight match, where the starting odds of the two teams are similar, but the first half in play stats point squarely towards a specific side, that side will be regarded as the favourite.

You will dutch the target scores above for 0.5pt. If there is no 2nd half goal you could lay the current score @1.40 for 0.5pt which will give you a scratch result with one late goal. No late goal means a loss of only 0.7pt. When you consider 47% of games have 2 second half goals the risk/reward is well in your favour.

As soon as the first second half goal goes in you have a decision to make. Trade some of the profit off one or both target scores, or let the game run and see where it ends. When the 2nd goal goes in trade out straight away to ensure a winning trade just in case a 3rd goal should come along. This is a simple, easy to understand and set up strategy, that will put you in a very strong position with just one goal.

* * *

The W2HTB Strategy

The W2HTB method, is also known as the "Half-Time Bomb strategy as you take up a position during half-time aiming to 'blow up' the goal markets in the later stages of the match. Only use this strategy when you have built up to a good level of experience. Do not be tempted to jump in with it before building up some experience in the markets. It is a brilliant strategy and good to have in your arsenal.

It's best to play this strategy aggressively. You should experience a high success rate with this method and good match reading skills can help increase the profits.

With the W2HB method we will be entering two markets at half time and playing them off against each other in the quest for a profit. If played right, a substantial profit can be made. I must stress that this strategy does require goals and I personally don't use a stop loss on it. If you choose to do the same, realise that the stake you decide to use may be lost in full if there are less than 2 goals in the second half.

The good news is that matches that are 0-0 at half time will have 2 goals in the second half about 47% of the time. The better news is that we may only need just a single goal to get into a "no-loss" break even position and we can expect at least 1 goal 78% of the time.

Entry Point

With the match 0-0 at the half time mark I will enter the over 1.5 goals and the over 2.5 goals market by splitting my stake into two parts.
I place 70% on over 1.5 goals along with the other 30% of my stake on over 2.5 goals.
For example, if my total stake was £100, I would be backing Over 1.5 Goals with £70 and Over 2.5 Goals with £30.

I'll then let the second half play out and be quite dynamic and ready to react when the goals start to go in. There are many different ways to play it out to maximise profits.

This strategy can obviously be used no matter what the scoreline is and you have to just adjust the goal markets you use accordingly.

For example, if it is 1-0, you will then use over 2.5 goals and over 3.5 goals. However, the optimal time to use this strategy and to be aggressive with it is when it is 0-0 and initially you should stick to this.

Usually if we can get a goal in the early stages of the second half, this can put us in a very strong position. The odds will drop low enough on both the over 1.5 and over 2.5 markets and this can give a nice profit when greened up right away. There is a more aggressive strategy though and I use it quite often.

I like to lay the same markets with the same stake I used to back, to give myself a risk free bet on over 1.5 goals and over 2.5 goals. This is usually around double the amount of profit that is available if greened. Of course there needs to be another goal, but it's still a break even if one doesn't materialise.

This is an ideal position. All you have to do is sit back and let the players do the work by getting the ball in the net. If you are a mature enough trader you will know it is brilliant to be in a position where you know you can no longer lose and it is just a matter of how much money you can then go on and make. The main reason for choosing this exit strategy is simply to make more money. You can double or triple your potential profits this way.

Even when the 2nd goal arrives, you may still have the option to green up on the over 2.5 goals market for a decent amount, depending on the amount of time left or the way the match is going. This is where match reading comes into it and you need to make a decision based on what see.

If the first goal arrives early in the second half, it is important to remember that you are in a position of strength and there is actually no rush to exit your position. More goals is good news and more profit.

I sometimes like to let the match play for a further 5 minutes for this very reason. This is usually because the markets can 'stick' for a short while immediately after a goal. This means the prices will not move away too quickly. Also, because you will be surprised at how quickly another goal can follow the first once the flood gates are opened.

If you have a strong favourite chasing a match with the score 1-1, then I would leave my free bet on over 2.5 goals open as they will be chasing down that 3rd goal. However, if that strong favourite was now leading the match 2-0, I may decide to lock in the profits. If I feel that team is strong enough to close out the match without conceding since they have no motive to chase further goals, then it's best to close the position and be happy with what we've got.

FULL TIME TRADING STRATEGIES

W10. (O/U1.5 Market).

I've had a good strike rate using this strategy taking the matches from the over 1.5 selections. All you need to do is back over 1.5 goals in two stages during the first half in-play.
You will Back over 1.5 goals @ 1.60 and 1.90 for 0.5 pt each.

1st Stage.
As soon as the price hits 1.60 enter and back over 1.5 goals for 0.5pt.
2nd Stage.
Back over 1.5 goals for .5pt. at 1.90. If a goal is scored in the meantime just let the first stage run. If you're matched at 1.90 you now have a 1pt liability and .75pt potential profit. That's a darn sight more than any banks interest rate.

Stay in if a goal is scored before 75'. You can trade out for scratch on both matched bets if the other goal doesn't happen.

If the game is still 0-0 at 75' equalise the loss across the overs and unders to reduce liability IF you can see from the in play stats that goals look unlikely. You'll notice that after 75' the odds reduce rapidly so your loss becomes greater as the game continues.

If a goal is scored by 60' you may wish to trade out for scratch, but check the in- play stats and if the game is open enough with plenty of action, consider staying in the trade for longer.

So many times we see goals in the selected markets coming before our back trades are matched so I've looked at way's to stop this happening.

Often and usually when a home favourite is involved, the over 1.5 odds may be as low as 1.20 or sometimes less. To overcome this and to give us a better chance to profit I recommend dripping your trade in until you've reach your maximum liability.

All you need do is to drip back over 1.5 goals at the following odds. These bets can be placed before kick off and the keep in play option makes sure that all we need to do is wait for them to be matched. Assuming a point is £10 place £2 @ 1.30, £2 @1.40, £3 @ 1.60 and finally £3 @ 1.90 and remember to click the KEEP in play button. After a goal you can cancel any unmatched. Some profit is better than no profit doing it this way.

Sometimes an early goal, within the first 5-10 minutes scuppers your trade. It happens and that is why the prices are low at KO. So think outside the box and instead of over 2.5 goals, try over 3.5 goals instead, especially if the game is listed as an over 2.5 with your selection process.

Recovery Trade

You can also use this **W10** strat as a recovery bet for a failed LTD1. We can expect 2 goals in the second half using of course your trade selections listing for O1.5 goals.

If using the **W10** as a recovery trade, then you won't green up or hedge across both outcomes. Also be aware that the price can take several minutes to settle after the 1st goal. So you have this option open to you when the first goal hits the net. If both teams are attacking and really trying to score I'd personally take this option off the table, as you only need one more goal for a full win during whatever time is left of the match.

And if you do intend to use this as a recovery trade then make certain that the first half in play stats warrant the risk and, you only cover the liability lost on the LTD1 trade.

TRADING O2.5 goals without stress or pressure.

This way of trading the over 2.5 goals market is a more conservative way of doing things. It's a relaxed and comfortable way to trade with a very low risk, but also a low profit potential. The up side of this is a very high strike rate of around 80%

It is a first half trade, that we will exit at half time or before, hopefully with a profit, but if not a reduced loss.

Here are some pointers to help you find the strongest selections possible.

1. Select matches that are between 1.75 - 1.85 on the Betfair over 2.5 goals market.

2. Select matches that are profiled as likely to produce over 2.5 goals from the stat site that you use.

3. Only use this strategy when you can actually see the game being played on a live stream. You do need to be able to see the game as it's being played and you need to take note of the following.

4. You need to see shots on target, at least one shot on target from either side.

5. You need to see attacking sides getting behind the defence and also note if they are organised going forward.

6. You need to see either or preferably both goalkeepers make a save.

7. You need to listen carefully to what the commentator is saying.

Is the way the game is being played exciting them. Is their voice raised? Are they praising players efforts? Do they sound downbeat?

Try and follow their match reading skills. They are a commentator and they should know the game and have profiled the match, so are in a good position to foresee what is going to happen.

With this being a conservative method of trading over 2.5 goals, we will not be staying in for the full match waiting for three goals. We will, or should be, greening up after the first goal.

THE STRATEGY

Don't open this trade if you are unable to watch and follow the game live. As 69% of all games across all leagues have a first half goal, this is a very strong basis to place your trade. With careful consideration of what is going on in the match and how things are panning out, we should be able to increase this percentage.

Watch and follow the game in play, take note of how the game is being played out taking into account all that I've mentioned in the numbered points above.

If you're happy with the way the game is being played at around the 15' Mark enter the trade by backing over 2.5 goals with 25% of a point.

Keep watching the game and if the game is showing plenty of action at the 25' mark and obvious intent from both sides, then and only then enter the second part of your trade by backing over 2.5 goals with another 25% of a point.

You now have 50% of your stake in the market and around 20' of game time left to play.

At this point you have 2 options.

Stop and don't put any more into the market if the game has slowed down or is not showing the same signs of a goal.

Or at around the 35' put in the remainder up to your liability, as long as the game is proceeding the way you like and a goal looks likely. Add another 50% of a point into the market. You have now committed 100% of your stake to the trade, now all you want is a goal. And there are 10' plus any stoppage time to get what we want.

When either team scores the price will of course drop so you can now trade out for a nice profit of between 40-65%. With this strategy you should trade out on the 1st goal no matter what time the goal came and no matter what stakes you have entered.

Profit is profit and at the end of the month every bit of it is important.

Should the game be 0-0 at HT (and it happens roughly 30% of the time) then trade out for a loss of approximately 40% of the stakes you have committed and move on to the next opportunity. So on a £10 full stake you've lost around £4, it's not going to hurt much, it's easily recovered. You'll find that by sticking to the pointers above you'll have more winning trades than losers and that means money in your bank.

Back O2.5 Goals Strategy. (Second strategy)

I always take my profit and recommend you do the same on the first goal.

Unless, there's a goal within the first 5' when this

happens I'll stay in and wait for another goal. If the underdog scores first it will not be worthwhile trading out as the price will hardly move. In this case I'll trade out straight away on the second goal. If it stays 1-0/0-1 at half-time trade out with a smaller profit or scratch. If the game has plenty of first half action, you may decide to stay in. We know most goals are scored in the 2nd half and so obviously, games that are drawn at half-time are won in the 2nd half. You will get better at spotting these opportunities when your match reading skills improve after watching lots of matches. You can always be ultra cautious at the start. There is absolutely nothing wrong with taking your profit at the earliest opportunity. Greed can be a profit killer.

I've also found that drip backing up to my max liability from say 1.85 up to when a goal is scored in the first half can work well. I keep drip backing in increments as the price improves. I'll start with a back bet at 1.85 then 2.05 then 2.30 and so on until my full liability is taken and matched.

Alternative Strategy O2.5 Goals. (Third strategy)

Using £100 per point I back over 2.5 goals at 2.0 for £72. This gives me £72 profit if it goes over

2.5 goals and a £72 loss if it does not.

What you do now is to use the other £28 to Back Under 1.5 goals.

If the game ends with less than 1.5 goals, I have a profit of £75 and if it goes over I have a loss of £28. (The amounts don't matter as long as it makes up 1 Point)

You can see I have covered myself, not completely, but partly*. The only way I can lose money on this game is if it ends 1-1, 2-0 or 0-2.

If it ends on one of those scores I will lose 1pt / £100, but I would have lost that anyway if I had just put the one bet on over 2.5 goals.

If the games ends 0-0, 1-0 or 0-1, then I will lose my £72 on the Over's but I will have a profit of around £75 on the Under 1.5 goals, so more or less scratch.

If the games does in fact go over 2.5 goals I will have a profit of £72 from that bet but a loss of £28 on the Under 1.5 goals. leaving an overall profit of £44.

You could also cover 0-1 /1-0 and 1-1 with your remaining £28 instead by dutching those scores. Just check out the prices at the time. Only use this strategy when you've got some trading time under your belt.

Adjust the above stakes downward to stay within your liabilities, I've used £100 as an example for ease of adjustment.

PLEASE NOTE It is impossible to fully cover your stake with any strategy that's ever been devised, the closest we can get is to partly cover our stake

W3.5

When assessing selections for this strategy, you need to look for two sides with a high first-half goal scoring record, along with a high second-half scoring record. Ideally you want two goals in the first half and two goals in the second half. Granted it's not easy to predict this, but we don't need all four goals to profit as I will explain.

Again using a liability of 1 point, before kick-off lay under 1.5 first-half goals for 50%, and also lay under 3.5 total match goals for 50%. We are covering the 1st half and full match markets

We are looking for a price between 1.3 and 1.8 but if I am confident I will take as high a 2.0. Normally you will find an average price of about 1.5 so our liability is half a point on each market.

Now we can just use this as a straight bet. If there are 2 or more first half and then 4 in the whole game we win 2 points.

If just one part of the trade wins then we still have small profit of £10.

But it's what we can do in play that is interesting.

Lets say there is an early first half goal. We could do any of the following on the first half goals market.

Green up.

Leave it and hope for a 2nd goal before half time as this will put us in a very strong position.

Leave it as it is with the intention of greening when we are at break even on the 1.5 goal market, meaning that we can then only lose the 3.5 lay.

Green the first half goal market. We should most of the time get enough green to cover our bets giving us a free shot at the over 3.5 part of the trade.

This is the option that I use most of all as I love having zero liability trades that offer the chance of a good return. A bet to nothing is the ideal scenario. What I try to do is get into this position of strength, and then I am free to move my profits about as I watch the game and make decisions based on what I see. Of course, this kind of trading does need a degree of experience.

The simple way of trading it is to green the the first half goal market after 1 goal and then green the total match goals market after 3 goals. Obviously all dependant on the time remaining.

There are literally loads of things that you can do in play depending on how the match is going. Lets face it some games are full on where it looks like a goal can be scored at any time. We can use this to our favour. I very rarely touch the 3.5 goal lay until there has been 3 goals, but if there are 2 early goals you could green up the 3.5 there and then for a very healthy profit.

The danger of this trade is the low scoring game. No goals in the first half and under 3 goals in the game will mean a full loss. However this shouldn't happen very often if your match selection process is correct. In virtually every game I have traded this way, I have had chances to at least break even/scratch.

LAY THE DRAW (Full Match)

Again you will find your selection from your research of the stats, and ideally we will look for matches with to have a strong home favourite. You'll also find that the kick-off price for the draw will be quite high because of this, so DO

NOT enter at kick-off at odds in excess of 5.0 Your maximum lay price should be no more than 4.0 or lower if possible.

This might sound scary, but of course, we will rarely lose all of our liability if our selection process is sound. There will be upsets of course, but we do have other options.

Laying the draw at KO we can place a back bet on the draw if it is 0-0 at half time, or we could place the back bet at 3.0 on the draw if no goals are scored before then. Bank protection is paramount.

We can always wait in play for the odds to come down before we LTD. I prefer to use this strategy as sometimes it takes even the strongest favourite a long time to break down an inferior teams stubborn defence. This way we can get very good low lay the draw odds from a match that looked like a stone cold solid home win pre-match.

Let's say we laid at 4.0 and no goals have been scored at 60 minutes. Now would be the time to look at getting out at around 2.0 by backing the draw and protecting our bank.

There's still 30' left to play though and if you're still happy with the way the game is being played out and the in-play stats are good, you may wish to stick with it until the first goal arrives.

The later the goal goes in the better for us from a profit point of view, especially if its the favourite that scores. If the underdog scores late on, it's not all bad news. There will be profit, but not as much as if the favourite scored.

The same applies if the underdog scores an early goal in the first half, I would usually trade out for a small loss and move on to the next trade.

Should the favourite take an early lead,or if they are showing more desire and intent to score, you may be more adventurous and expect them to go 2 up. In this case your profit will be greater. Always bear in mind though that you are gambling with your green.

If a there is a red card, and especially if it goes to the home team, I'm out of the trade.

The only exception I make is if the away side has the red and the home side has shown more intent to score and peppering the goal with shots.

In summary, it is always better NOT to enter above 4.0. Wait in play for the price to drop. If it's 0-0 at HT and the in-play stats are good enough to suggest getting involved, do so with confidence.

Your exit should never be varied. Your plan

should be to stick to your stop loss and green. Hedge up on the 1st goal.

Full time 3 Goals needed correct Score strategy WFT3

With this version you are only backing two score-lines 1-2 and 2-1, so you need both teams to score.

Your maximum risk is only 0.5pt and there is very little to do in-play. This is a conservative correct score strategy that has medium risk/high reward. Always be aware of in play stats and wait while watching the game for the prices available to become more agreeable. For me this is usually aroud the 20 minute mark.

What we do not want with the WFT3 strategy are early goals. It only takes a couple of goals for us to be right on top of our set up target scores, so 0-1/1-0 at half-time is ideal. This is good enough reason to be patient and not to open the trade too early in the match. First half goals are the ruin of this trade.

If you decide to wait for better prices and enter trades after 15-20' It is unlikely that the half-time score will be more than 0-1/1-0. Delaying your entry point reduces your risk and can increase the profits from well researched matches.

The maximum loss for this trade will only ever be 0.5 points and it is very simple to set up. There are a dutching calculators freely available on the web or it can be done on the Betfair site itself.

Dutch the 2-1 and 1-2 scoreline's for a total of 0.5pt. A fast method of dutching is on Betfair, add both scorelines to the bet slip and choose 'stake'. Enter your stake and confirm. Betfair will automatically place your dutched bets.

To try out this method, go to Betfair, choose any football match, go to correct scores and try the above instructions. Just take note of the 'What If' alongside the selected scores.

After kick-off, there is no need to do any trading at all until the game hits 1-1, or either of the two target scoreline's occur. You'll get a good green on 1-1 in the 2nd half depending on how long the match has to play out, but remember you're just 1 goal away from your target score, so don't completely hedge out, just reduce your liability.

This is a simple way to trade correct scores with very little work to do. This is the way I love to trade. Less work for more profit. This strategy can also be a set and forget bet with a maximum loss of just .5Pt

Remember that we are traders and profit matters. Reducing risk whenever possible should always be our goal. If after watching the game it doesn't look like that the goals we are hoping for will be forthcoming, get out of the trade.

There is also another option.

Insurance Trade to cover WFT3

We can set up and use the W10 strategy trade as a safety net, so if the game fails to hit our target scores we will make scratch should the game end with only 2 goals. i.e 1-1/2-0/0-2. Bear in mind if the game gets to 1-1 and you decide to take your green you win twice. Take a look at the W10 instructions from earlier and remember you're only looking to cover your stake on the WFT3 trade.

After looking at games where the half-time score was 1-1, I noticed that by dutching 2-1/1-2 at that score the results can be improved. Obviously the profit isn't as great when only one more goal is needed, but delaying placing the dutch for as long as you dare can increase the returns. Keep in mind most goals are scored in the second half, so maybe consider 1-3/3-1 depending of course who is on top of the game according to the in play stats. You do need to follow the game in play and check the in play stats at HT to see if there's been plenty of action and especially attempts on goal, corners etc.

If the match hits 2-1/1-2 before 75', trade out for profit by laying the current score. It won't be more than 30-40% but its better than 0% return if it goes 3-1/1-3 or 2-2. Also if the score is 1-1 at HT and you decide to enter then, you could also back 2-2 for a small amount to cover all your liabilities and give yourself some profit if that's the final score.

After 75' stay in play. If its still 1-1 (your stake is covered if you used the W10 trade) all you can hope for is a another goal, so as to hit the target score. You're in a good position. In this situation using WFT3 I would stay in and expect target score to come in.

You can scratch or green up depending upon when or if the next goal arrives. It is advisable to take your profit no matter how much time is left. It takes seconds to score a goal and many a good profit has disappeared from traders screens thanks to an added time goal. If it stays 1-1 and you've not greened up, take it on the chin. It happens. If you know that you played the trade as you should have given the stats, and the evidence of your own eyes, then you did the right thing. It's not your fault if some of the players were goal shy.

Extra insurance instead of the above could be to back 0-0 in the correct score market. This wont cost much, as the odds will be good and you can cover your liability and green up if it gets to half time goalless.

When the first goal is scored, back the draw in the match odds market. You must be highly selective when using insurance trades, as every penny you insure with lessens your overall profit.

The above is the simplest way to trade this strategy. Please make sure you fully understand the principles and what affects prices and how time decay works before you venture fully into correct score trading.

BTS

This both teams to score strategy, aka BTTS, Both Teams To Score, BTS is my favourite way to trade. It is played in 3 stages. Pre-match and after a goal is scored. Dutch the following in the correct score market. 1-2, 1-3, 2-1, 3-1 for half a point.

Lay under 4.5 Goals as insurance for your full stake of 1Pt.

The lay odds will be around 1.25 and ideally you want this price lower, so put a lay bet in of 1.18 to 1.20 and set to keep in play.

When the first goal is scored, and not before, back the draw in the match odds market for the remaining stake (if the U4.5 was 1.13) then use the remainder to back the draw.

I will explain this using £100 as a point.

1. Dutch 1-2, 1-3, 2-1, 3-1 for £50 (0.5 point)

2. Put a lay into the queue on U4.5 goals for £100 (1 point) at no more than 1.20 ideally as low as you can get matched). That will be £20, 0.2 of a point, of liability.

3. That will leave us with £30 (0.3) to back the draw in the match odds market after the 1st goal

You can adjust your staking in proportion to the figures given above.

If an early goal is scored and your U4.5 Lay doesn't get matched take the red and get out of the trade. Again take it on the chin.

You may also consider a lay of U3.5 instead of U4.5. Although this is more expensive, if there is a goal fest and the game has more than 5 goals, you win twice.

That's it. The only danger is if BTS doesn't

happen, in other words, if there's a 0 in the scoreline at full time (1-0/0-1 2-0/0-2 etc.) the trade is lost.

If both teams score, we have everything covered, if the game goes 3-3 we will profit twice with the U4.5 lay and the draw.

The 80' Lay

This is a very low-risk, high-profit strategy which is essentially more of a straight 'set and forget' bet.

As long as you stick to the rules you will find that you will make regular profits.

Probable selections are for any game, but not friendlies. Look for games where both teams have something to play for, or you are watching the match and both teams are eager to win.

All you are looking for are games with the following scorelines at the 70-minute mark. 1-0/0-1/1-1.

The LTD price in match odds will be around the same as the 1-1 correct score price, so it makes much more sense to lay the correct score rather than laying the draw.

Laying the correct score means that once a goal is scored you win and your out with your profit.

All you need to do is lay any of the above correct scores sticking to the rules below. Do not deviate from them. We want as little risk as possible.

Rules:

Find your selections at around the 70 minute mark.

Check the 'in play' stats for BOTH sides. You want both sides to be active and showing intent. Between 70'- 80 minutes, before entering, watch the live stream or graphic to ensure there is plenty of action, ideally from both sides, but as long as one of the sides is dominating and going for a goal you can go ahead and enter. On Betfair check the stats for the past 5, 10 and 15 minutes. You're looking for high numbers of shots, shots on target and corners within those time frames.

When you are satisfied that there is enough going on in the match, lay 0.5Pt at 1.40 on any of these scoreline's 1-0/0-1/1-1. This price usually appears around the 80 minute mark. Using 1Pt = £100, lay £50 @1.40. The liability is therefore £20.

As you are watching the game play out, and you're still happy with the fact that both or either side are going for a goal and the goals hasn't been scored, enter again and lay another 0.5Pt @ 1.20, liability will be £10. So now you're fully in for 1Pt with a liability or potential loss of just

0.3pt for a profit potential of 1.0pt.

There is absolutely no problem putting your lays into the queue. In fact its a good idea. you will usually find your bet matched, even when the prices are showing a few ticks above your entry price on the Betfair page.

As always, you can drip in your total liability in increments, from whatever price you are happy with. If you can see that both teams are trying to score, the odds might not move as quickly as they would in a match without as much goal scoring intent, so it is good to get some money in at least.

This is a high risk strategy, but being highly selective with the matches that you choose to enter, the low risk versus high returns mean that this can be a very profitable tactic.

✳ ✳ ✳

Trading Correct Scores

This first part is absolutely essential to your success. If you fail to grasp these essentials you will not succeed at Trading Correct Scores.

Odds Movements:

Very Strong Home Favourite:

If we have a game involving a strong favourite at home, you'll find the odds on offer are around 1.3 or shorter. Then generally while no goals are scored, 0-0, 0-1, 1-0 and 2-0 will all begin to move in from kick-off. The 3-0 scoreline may also move in a little, depending on the amount of action within the game. The 1-1, 2-1 and 1-2 score lines should remain relatively static, whilst all the others will steadily go out, some quicker than others.

If there are still no goals by 40 minutes, then 2-0 will start to move out, although 1-1 should still hold relatively stable. The 0-0, 1-0 and 0-1 scores will continue to come in. By 50 minutes, the 1-1 will start to move out, and ten minutes later, the 1-0 and 0-1 will also reverse their trends and start back out. The 0-0 scoreline of course continues to come in.

If the strong home side score in the first 15 minutes of the match, then 1-0 will go out slightly (as further goals are expected), 2-0 and 3-0 and any unquoted (AU) will shorten, 2-1 will stay static, while 1-2 will fly out. If the away side score first inside 15 minutes, then 0-1 shortens dramatically, as does 0-2, 2-1 and 1-1. The 3-1 scoreline also shortens somewhat, whilst AU doesn't move much at all.

Evenly-matched sides:

Let's look at the same scenarios for evenly-matched teams. The 0-0, 1-0 and 0-1 score lines will move in, as usual. The 1-1 score will remain largely static, as will 2-0 and 0-2 (maybe some slight shifts either way), but the 2-1 and 1-2 score lines will head out.
Around the 30-35 minute mark, 2-0 and 0-2 will begin moving out.
1-1 will also start moving away, but at a slower pace. If the home side score inside 15 minutes, then 1-0 will shorten, as will 1-1, 2-0, 2-1 and 2-2. 1-2 will lengthen slightly. AU will shorten. If the away side score first, the reversible score lines shorten (0-2, 1-2.)

* * *

Okay, so knowing generally how the odds move, let's now look at some of the most popular strategies. Unfortunately, despite their multitude, there are no methods or strategies, that I know of that can guarantee a profit each and every time. Some are high risk, and some provide a hedged level of safety, but all can win and all can lose, depending on the situation.

Strategies:

Laying 0-0

I suppose we had better get this one out of the way first. It's not much of a strategy, but this infamous bet has attracted the same kind of attention and notoriety as its match odds counterpart, Lay The Draw. It's certainly the most well-known, and probably the most commonly-struck bet of any kind in the correct score market. It also seems to be heralded and derided in equal measure, often dividing opinion amongst the betting community.

The reason it's so popular is that it's quick, easy and enticingly, feels like it could be the road to easy riches. As we all know, football matches are all about goals. So surely guessing and betting that at least one goal will be scored is a good idea? Well, perhaps.

The most obvious problem of course is what happens when no goals are forthcoming; the bettor then faces a total wipe-out of their stake. Furthermore, it should be borne in mind that the given odds for any particular match will generally be an accurate reflection of that scoreline being achieved. Betfair markets are notoriously efficient, so it's probably not a good idea just to say to yourself, "Ooh, I can lay this at 9s, I'll have some of that," because you've made no evaluation of whether this constitutes value or not.

Lay the 0-0 scoreline in the French Second division (Lique 2) and the odds can be as low as 7 or 8. Lay the same scoreline in a match involving Barcelona at home, and you can often be looking at lay odds of 25 to 30. Which one is value? Probably neither. The question then is, would you be willing to risk £2,500 or more just to win £100? I certainly wouldn't.

So, blind laying of the 0-0 will almost certainly lead to the poor-house, but could there be any situations where this can actually be a good bet? Well, the answer is yes, of course there are. For example, let's suppose you have a match where the starting odds quickly decay after kick-off. But then the home team start playing magnificently, hammering the away side into submission, hitting the woodwork and getting involved in a rush of goalmouth melees.

Well you may feel that laying 0-0 under those circumstances is a decent option. And I might tend to agree with you.

In the past I have personally laid 0-0 when this kind of scenario is playing out, and I'm sure I will do so again in the future. But either way – and be under no illusions here - this is straight betting and NOT trading, and the risk already outlined above will always be there.

The Assessed Lay of 0-0

Perhaps not that much better than the blind version of this bet, but by analysing the stats to see who starts games slowly, who scores for fun in the second-half of games and who concedes easily as their fitness begins to falter, are avenues to explore that can only help to improve your hit-rate when laying 0-0.

You could also use Poisson to calculate the percentage chances of each scoreline being achieved. If you do utilise pure Poisson, you should ensure that you increase the probability of 0-0 and 1-1, and reduce the probability of a 1-0 home win and a 0-1 away win. This is because the Poisson model is known to under forecast 0-0 and 1-1 draws and over forecast 1-0 and 0-1. There are also other well-known algorithms that you could use to calculate the goal expectation and, again, these would all help you to make a more reasoned decision for you to lay 0-0.

The Time-limited Lay of 0-0

Some people believe that, whilst there may be no real value in a straight lay of the 0-0 scoreline, there might just be some value for a limited duration. Different periods of a match have different likelihoods of goals being scored, so directing a lay towards those periods could prove profitable.

The idea here is to set a maximum liability for all bets of this type, and then to place a lay of 0-0 someway through the match, starting at the optimal time for goals to be scored. This lay stays in place until the defined liability is reached, at which point the bet is reddened-up. If a goal is scored whilst the lay is in place then obviously the bet is won.

This bet is favoured by some due to its targeted

nature and for its defined liability, managing risk a little more wisely than a straight lay of 0-0.

Other Time-related bets

Placing bets within the correct score market for a defined period of time is not only restricted to the 0-0 scoreline. For closely-matched sides or when the goal expectation is low, another common approach is to back the 0-0, 1-0 and 0-1 score lines.

When in-play, the odds for all these score lines will shorten, providing a trader with an opportunity to green-up after fifteen or twenty minutes. Some traders even wait until half-time before greening-up.
An early goal will of course blow two parts of this bet out of the water, leaving the trader with a red position, but this will be dramatically less than any lay of 0-0.

Backing 0-0

If you back 0-0 (perhaps using the scalping techniques detailed below) and lay off the same amount a few ticks later, this can provide you with a free bet on this scoreline. From this advantageous position, you then have a few

options. You can either leave it there and hope for the game to finish 0-0, you can
watch the odds drop further, allowing you to green-up a reasonable figure across all score lines, or you could wait for the odds on 0-0 to drop further and then lay that scoreline using only the green you have on 0-0 as your risk.

Additionally, this could be used as insurance on an in-play trade of other score lines.

This technique can also be used pre-match for a considerably lower risk. If it is felt the 0-0 scoreline odds are too large, then this can be backed with the hope that it will steam before the start of the match. Indeed this is a very popular strategy not just for the 0-0 scoreline but for several others.

Sometimes a goal fest is forecast and the high score lines can get overpriced, but as the match draws closer, a more reasoned view is taken which can cause all these larger score lines to shorten.

Again, the trader can either green-up across all score lines or use the green they have on a particular score to use in-play.

* * *

Dutching

This is backing all score lines that are most likely to happen for an even profit. If for example, the market is expecting a home win in a game with two goals or less, then a dutch of 0-0, 1-0, 0-1, 2-0 and 2-1 may be made, ensuring the same profit whichever one of these score lines the game finishes on.

The advantage of this bet is that you cover a lot of ground, but the disadvantage is that the more ground you cover (the larger the percentage of the book), then the greater the risk-to-reward ratio becomes.

You should also be careful about backing too many score lines, an Overs or Under's bet could prove to be better value.

Dutching can be used in many ways, using any selection of score lines that you want. Trial-and-error is the best way forward using the information on odds movements that I've already provided.

A home win with a high goal expectation? Then you could Dutch 2-0, 2-1, 3-0, 3-1 and AU (Any Unquoted).

* * *

Looking for a trade at a later date? Back 0-0 (as an insurance bet only), along with 1-1, 2-1 and 1-2. When the market moves out further, also back 2-2. These are basic examples, but come up with your own if you can. You're going to need to be able to think outside the box, and this will come with experience of trading correct scores.

For some, dutching is a staple correct score bet. It also has the advantage that you can trade-out of it after a defined period of time, or the bet can be left to run.

The Tracker

No, this is nothing to do with mortgages, but more to do with tracking the current score and the two next possible scores along.

With the average number of goals scored around 2.5, this strategy is often utilised after two goals are scored. At that point the current score and the next two possible scores along are backed.

Greening-up or selecting additional score lines is then a matter of reacting to events within the match, which of course means the match should be watched whilst trading.

* * *

The Home Win Predictor

With ten or fifteen minutes remaining in the match, the match is drawn or the home team has a goal advantage. The away team has its back to the wall as the home team continually surge forward, seeking another goal.

You can see that either the away team will hold-out or the home team will pinch a late goal. Okay, so dutch the current score and the next home win scoreline – but weigh the current scoreline so that you have a scratched position should there be no further goals.

The obvious risk here is when, against the run of play (and how many times have we heard that phrase?), the away team run up the other end and score a surprise goal. Under those circumstances you would have a full loss of stake.

The 1-1 Trade

What if the strong favourite playing at home go a goal behind early in the game? What should we do? What happens to the odds when this happens? After the market is back open, the current scoreline will settle where the 0-0 was before the goal, and gradually begin decaying in the same manner. Laying this is essentially the same as laying 0-0 at that point. But what about 1-1? What happens to that?

Well, the market strongly fancies an equaliser, so 1-1 will begin decreasing nicely in price. This provides an opportunity to trade with less risk than the lay of 0-0. Backing 1-1, especially if the home side are attacking causes a decent drop in price, allowing you to lay it off later.

If the home side do equalise and you have an open position in the market, then this will lead to even greater profits. The risk here is a second goal from the underdog, but you can either live with this risk or else place a small covering bet on the away team's next score.

The 2-0 Scalp

This popular strategy is a reasonably safe way to scalp the correct score market of a match with a strong home favourite. From kick-off, this price will start to come in, so backing first and laying off a few ticks later should yield decent profits whilst also offering you the greater possibility of having an open position when or if the home team score.

* * *

This will then lead to greater profits. The risk is the same as many of these strategies; and that's if the away team should score first. If you have an open position during such an event you'll suffer a full loss.

Scalping however is about getting into the market at the right time (i.e. when the away team do not have the ball).

The Current Score Scalp

Bank Health Warning!
Scalping in this way tracks the current score, with the idea being to take a few ticks here and there. The importance of this type of trading is to have an open position in the match for as short a time as possible (or for as long a time as possible when there is no risk but the odds are still falling). The no risk periods are shots ballooned over the bar, substitutions and injuries.

The difficulty arises when you open a position and find yourself unable to close it properly due to sudden action. As I've just mentioned, this is high-risk trading and should be performed with a large measure of caution.

Betfair Correct Score markets are generally 2%

above (for backs) or 2% below (for lays) a 100% book. This is the over round, which is much less than with the high street bookies.

To complete a profitable book you either need to back all the selections under 100% or lay them all over 100%. Some people back those score lines that will inevitably steam once the match gets underway, and then back the remaining ones that should drift to higher odds than are currently available. In other words, they put an offer in for those driftable scores and wait for their odds to get matched.

This should be done without clicking the keep bets option. If a goal is scored before being matched on all score lines, then it would not advisable to leave money in place, that will be snapped up, for score lines that cannot ever occur. If all selections are eventually matched, however, then you will have completed your book at less than 100% for a guaranteed profit.

The Alternative

A selection of correct scores can also be satisfactorily used to replace another market entirely than the one you were originally intending to back or lay, only with greater value. Let's say that you have assessed a match as a low-scoring home win and you want to back under 2.5 goals; well this could perhaps be replaced by backing 0-0, 1-1, 1-0 and 2-0 instead. By leaving the out the 0-1 and 0-2 score lines from the equation, you are of course increasing your risk but you are also potentially increasing your profit using a judgement on how the game may be played out.

The correct score market can also be used in conjunction with other markets. Backing or laying a correct score, or several correct scores, effectively negates the possibility of some other event occurring in other markets, which could be used to your advantage. Using this pick-'n'-mix approach, it's possible to work-out a comfortably hedged position. So what do I mean by this?

Well, if you back the 1-0 scoreline on the full-time correct score market, then you are also effectively saying that (as an example) a half-time correct score of 0-2 will not occur.
The two are mutually exclusive. You may not actually be thinking this precise thing when making your bet, but if your bet wins then the half-time 0-2 has to fail.
As it happens, in this particular instance the reverse is also true.

* * *

If you back the full-time correct score of 2-1, then backing home win-both-halves absolutely cannot succeed. Any win-both-halves bet can only succeed if the full time score is two goals or greater.
Or if you back the full-time correct score of 1-1 then you have, in essence, also bet against, without actually placing a bet against a half-time/full-time back of home/home.

Using this logic, we can then think of a Correct Score bet as a kind of "soft backing or laying" of selections in another market. These may be useful to you. For example, the three most common results in the half-time/full-time market are Home/Home, Draw/Home and Away/Away.

If you are interested in dutching these three by all means do so, but you could also consider backing the first two along with 0-1, 0-2 and 1-2 instead. Could this lead to greater profits? You'll have to work that out for yourself, but either way you can see how certain score lines can replace or cover selections in other markets.

This pick 'n' mixing of different markets to build-up a position can be extremely powerful if given a bit of thought. Many of your ideas here will ultimately be negated by the powerful accuracy and efficiency of the markets, and by the countless bots out there scouring the markets to close-up profitable positions.

But if you're creative and able to look at these cross-market opportunities using an abstract perspective, then there may yet still be opportunities waiting to be taken advantage of. It's just up to you to find them.

Summary:

The main issue here is that the correct score market has huge potential, and for every strategy that you can come up with for a single scoreline, there are a dozen others waiting to be considered.

So the message must be to take some time and carefully consider all the options available to you. It's a fabulous market to get involved with and can provide a good degree of satisfaction if you can master it, or conjure up your own winning strategy.

You now understand price movements and what happens when an event occurs or through time decay. If you don't understand, then proceed no further because you're wasting your time. Go back to the start of this chapter and read it again until you do.

So what we have is a correct score trading strategy, with cover options to take in play, which will reduce the likelihood of losses. Of course losses cannot be totally avoided, but I've set out the steps you can take in play to lessen the loss and increase your chance to make a profit. Again, if you don't understand how price movements are affected by events and time decay do not proceed any further until you do, it is so important you fully understand it.

WWW

This strategy involves backing three correct scores, 1-1, 2-1 and 1-2 and is based on the most popular scorelines by means of averages.

When assessing matches for this strategy, I check two markets before looking at the correct score odds. Firstly, I'm looking for match odds of no lower than 1.8 for the favourite, and I'm also looking at under 2.5 goals odds being around 1.9 - 2.1.

If these criteria are met, you will find more often than not, that 1-1 is trading at between 7 and 8.5 and the other two at about 11-13.
I would then usually back 1-1 for about 1.5 x the amount I'm backing the other two for, so £2 on 2-1 and £2 on 1-2 with £3 on 1-1, gives a total of £7.
Another staking example would be £5 on 1-1, and £2.50 each on 2-1/1-2 giving a total of £10.
If the game is still 0-0 after half an hour I normally look to put a small amount on 2-2 at 25.0-30.0

What can go wrong?

When assessing any correct score trades I think

it's sensible to look at what might go wrong and by so doing to assess your 'danger scores'. We can then work out how to deal with them.

The first, and most distressing danger is the dreaded bore score draw, the 0-0. The easiest way I've found to alleviate the pain caused by this scoreline is by scalping it pre-match, trying to pinch 1 or 2 ticks. By trading pre-match your stake itself is safe, the only danger is that the price moves against you rather than for you.

My experience shows that if you back 0-0 with about 30 to 45 minutes to go you will usually get at least one tick movement.

There are no guarantees but often I can get between £35 and £50 'free' sitting on 0-0.

In-play you can either just leave your money sitting on 0-0 or lay some of it off as the price of 0-0 drops.

There are only really two other main dangers; first that no goal is scored until very late in the game and the 1-1 price doesn't come in enough to lay it off profitably. Secondly, two goals come very early in the game, again resulting in insufficient price movements. An absolute goal fest at any time is always a possibility, but if you are nervous about that, why not look at taking some cover in the under and over goal markets?

* * *

In-play trading

There are a number of ways this strategy can be traded in-play. In an ideal world the game would play out thus: The dogs score first, bringing the 1-1 in. The favourites equalise at about 60 minutes enabling a green of 1-1 to cover all stakes and give a profit on all scores.
Then you can either green up across the board, or wait for a 1-2 or 2-1. At this stage you are effectively laying the draw with absolutely no downside.
If you'd had the foresight to back 2-2 as well as the other scores you'd be laughing all the way to the bank if 2-1 or 1-2 comes before the 80th minute! That's the ideal and it happens surprisingly often.
There are danger points to consider though, and you need to have a plan.

Two quick goals bringing the score to 0-2 or 2-0 can be tricky as two thirds of your trade is gone in a flash. There's little you can do here, except to hedge your remaining bet and walk away, or you could stand firm if you're prepared for the fact that 3-0 or 0-3 (or staying the same until the end) will lose your entire stake.

Another precaution might be to take a small bet

on the next goal mark, or if those goals are early in the game you could lay over 2.5 goals at a very low price to guard against the game staying the same.

The game is 0-0 at half time...and you have no 0-0 cover as discussed above. Two choices really. Hedge for a small loss or stand firm and hope for goals second half. You could consider backing 0-0 1-0 0-1 maybe to cover your stakes. Use the 'what-if' on BF to see how to stake, but it will eat a lot of your potential profit!

The game is 0-0 at 80 mins and you have no 0-0 cover, consider hedging for a larger loss, and maybe lay 0-0 for the red amount, it obviously increases your exposure but if the game is won 1-0 or 0-1 puts you in a scratch position.

There are other banana skins, but the beauty of this trade, when it works, is that the return is generally pretty good.

Always make certain the match is going in play on the exchange or you won't be able to trade out. If your trading cup, qualifying or competition matches without good pre match stats and especially with 2 legged matches your risk is far greater. These matches are more volatile due to us having to figure out a teams motivation for the game, rested players etc. Tread carefully here.

One final important point I need to bring up is liquidity. It is very important because if you've entered a market where there's little money involved, you will not be able to trade out. Always check that the money in the market allows you to trade the way you want, given your stake size.

How much liquidity is enough?
There must be at least £5000 to be reasonably sure you'll be able to trade out. The majority of the major European/Asian leagues i.e. EPL, Bundesliga, La Liga, SerieA, China SL, Japan J, Korean K as well as Nth/Sth. American leagues etc. will usually have more than enough so they shouldn't be a problem.

So just be fully aware of the danger of not enough money available to get matched before you enter a trade if trading outside the main leagues

SUMMARY

Evenly matched games, the home side no lower than 1.80 and under 2.5 at around 2.0
Set an amount of money as a % of bank you are

prepared to LOSE, work the rest of your plan out with that figure in mind.

Try to get some free money on 0-0 pre-match, Stakes should be around a straight dutch on 1-1 1-2 2-1 if 0-0 at 25' put a small amount on 2-2 If a goal is scored I would usually try to lay half my total stakes on the 1-1 scoreline UNLESS the dog scores against the run of play.

1-1 is where the payday starts. Green completely on 1-1 will probably give an overall green on all scores. Then you can either let the other 2/3 ride for a while, or hedge all bets and go down the pub or move on to the next game!

0-0 HT a) hedge for small loss or b) stand firm or c) cover 0-0 1-0
0-1 or maybe even lay under 0.5.
0-0 80 mins hedge for larger loss (unless 0-0 1-0 and 0-1 covered) and maybe lay 0-0 to cover that loss..

The most important thing to remember is this:

If a trade goes against you - DO SOMETHING POSITIVE to reduce your liabilities and losses. Don't sit there like a rabbit in the headlights. Think outside the box. Are there any other markets that might come to your rescue?

***

Scalping

An essential weapon in the traders armoury, it is advisable to learn this technique thoroughly. It offers instant cover against any liabilities you have on any trade. But a warning here. Do not attempt any form of scalping until you have a good understanding of how markets and prices are affected by events including time decay.
Selection criteria: The following markets are the best for scalping:
Under 1.5/2.5 goals.
Current Correct score.
Current Next score.
Draw in match odds.

The under 1.5 is a personal favourite for scalping. On an average game the under 1.5 price will be around 3.6 to back. By half time this price will have halved if the score is 0-0, in fact the under 1.5 will be the same, (or near as) at half time as the starting price of the under 2.5.
So let's consider this, if it starts at 3.6 then it will drop around 40 ticks per 10 mins on average to reach it's 1.8 at half time.
So what is the best way to use this information?

Looking across all the European leagues down to

the third levels, in around 12.5% of matches there will have a goal in the 1st 15 minutes which equates to 1 game in 8, which is pretty good odds in our favour!

What else helps with scalping?

Live games that you are watching are a must.
Trading blind is far too risky.
How do you know where the ball is?
How do you know what is happening in the game?
Have there been many chances?

To trade blindly really should be avoided.
Even streamed matches have various delays of between 10 seconds and 2 minutes.
Look for the gaps in the market, spaces between odds. This will be similar once the game goes in play.
Whilst trading a live game on Friday with regards to the under 1.5 market, these are the trades I placed.
The game was an African Nations game and about 5 minutes had been played and score was still 0-0. The price on the under 1.5 was 3.20. A back was submitted at 3.20 which was quickly matched. I put in a lay at 3.10, 2 ticks lower. This was taken within 30 seconds at a point of

the game where the ball was in the goalkeepers hands and was safe.

There was very little money in the queue so the lay bet was going to be taken quickly as it was at the front.

Then I resubmitted at 3.05 to back after spotting very little money below this and big gaps in the market. Once taken the lay side was again submitted at 2.94 and taken within a minute. Lastly the price drop from 2.90 to 2.54 took about 45 seconds a very nice scalp.

So in summary:

The first 15 minutes are safest.

Look for the gaps, try for better prices and once bet taken instantly resubmit on lay side 2 or 3 ticks lower. When the price is over 3.0 the price increments are in .5s so using £50 stakes you will make £2.50 per tick made or £1 for £20 stakes which is 2.5 times better than when the price drops below 3.0.

IF you do get caught you're not totally out of it as 2 goals are needed for you to lose your stake.

By being at the front of the queue you will be matched quicker.

Whilst liquidity is important in any market, gaps and getting bets matched quickly happens more regularly in the under 1.5 market.

Scalping under 2.5

This is a safer method where a goal won't be as costly, but the drops of course will not be as quick. In the 1st 10 minutes of a game the drops can be anything up to 25 ticks!
Even 1 goal isn't a disaster because at HT, or within 5-10 mins of the start of the second half, you should still make a scratch trade or a small survivable loss.

Gaps are not as apparent due to more liquidity and under 2.5 scalping is a favourite for many traders.

Scalping the 0-0

This can pay handsome dividends. More so when the price is over 10 and a £20 back and lay 1 tick scalp can give you £10 green on the 0-0 scoreline. Scalping only early on into a game is recommended for this reason. Of course getting caught on 0-0 will lose your stakes. Perhaps consider using it with a back on the 2-0 and 0-2 score lines to give you some insurance in case of a goal.

* * *

Scalping the 1-0 and 0-1

The beauty of this is that both prices will come in for majority of the 1st half. When a goal is scored and when the scores have been scalped simultaneously, you will lose on one but there's a good chance the price on the other will come in to allow you to hedge out.

Conclusion

Scalping and using it as insurance on another trade makes sense. If you're new to scalping, try smaller stakes and learn to nip in and out, get in and out as quickly as possible. The less time you're in, the less risk there is of being caught on the wrong side of a scoreline.
Look for the gaps in the market and where the amounts to trade are small. As soon as your back bet is taken, submit on the lay side straight away. Being at the front of the queue means less time and less risk.

Sometimes the games you were intending to get into are postponed, or perhaps the first goal is scored too early. Do not try and replace it with another game that you have not researched!

Be patient and wait for the right opportunities to

come along.

Again remember, "a trading market is where the patient make and take money from the impatient".

Don't Over Trade

It is very easy to be tempted into too many trades. Over trading will inevitably lead to long term losses, so don't give in to that temptation. You have a plan, stick to it and do not be tempted to deviate from your plan.
I once conducted an experiment, one Friday evening on the Dutch Eerste (2nd Division) a league that is usually good for goals.
Using my software, I traded 15 games simultaneously with two markets on each game, FHG and O2.5 goals, it was madness!
Goals were flying in everywhere, no sooner had I hedged one than I had to hedge another game. It was a crazy 45 minutes and the result was I made 7.5 Pt's. But was it worth it? For the profit yes it was, for the pressure and stress no it wasn't. I took a lot away from having done those trades.

Stake sensibly.

* * *

Your stake will be relative to the size of your bank. It would be incredibly foolish to go into any trade with liabilities too big for your bank, so don't be one of those fools!

On the other hand, your stake should not be too small either as this means you are not making your bank work for you.

Divide your bank into 100 Pt's and work from there. And do not under ANY circumstances exceed your set liabilities.

Limit losses.

Quite often you will be in a trade that is going wrong. The only thing to do is accept that fact and trade out for a smaller loss than you would suffer if you were to stay in. By doing that, you can look upon a loss as a win because you have not lost as much as you would have done.

Compound as you go.

Einstein was right when he said, "compounding is the 8th wonder of the world." By increasing your bank you will also be increasing your stake size, thus making your wins bigger and growing your bank even faster. It is quite incredible how quickly a bank can grow by using this method.

* * *

Month 1:
You start with a bank of £1,000 and divide it into 100 Pts.
Therefore, the value of 1Pt is £10. When you hit your profit target of 10 points, at the end of the month your bank stands at £1,100.

Month 2:
You once again divide your bank into 100 Pts which means that now the value of 1Pt is £11. You hit your 10% profit target again and your bank stands at £1,210.

Month 3:
1pt is now worth £12.10 and hitting your 10pt profit target grows your bank to £1,331.

Month 4:
1Pt is worth £13.31 and your bank grows to £1,464.10 when you hit your profit target of 10Pt, and so on. By the time you reach the end of year one, your £1,000 bank has become £3,138.43
At the end of year two it is up to £9,849.73. After just three years, your £1,000 bank has now grown into £30,912.68
In case you have not realised already, 10Pt profit per month is a very achievable amount. It works out at roughly 0.3Pt per day, so during your first month you are looking to make just £3 profit per

day. Do you think you can do that?

A 10Pt profit per month is all it takes to grow £1,000 into £30,000 after three years. You're now a big fan of compounding, right?
Your biggest enemy is impatience. Stick to 10Pt's per month and don't be tempted to push your luck. Make sure you record your trades and stick to the aim of steady, consistent bank growth per month.
If you give in to temptation, you may well spiral out of control and blow your bank. Don't do it. There is a lot to learn about trading, so take your time, be patient and keep the pressure and stress off yourself at all times. The skills you learn as you go along will last you a lifetime. You will never be without a means of income as long as the betting exchanges continue to flourish. This looks like a gimme as more and more people forsake the high street bookies and latch on to the value of betting exchanges

Bank management is critical to your progression. If you are unable to control your funds then you will not stay in the market very long at all, and all your work will have been for nothing. Your bank is your working capital; it is all you have to work with so it has to be protected at all times. Do your research, make your daily trading plan, stick to that plan, stake sensibly, and take profits at each opportunity, and also aim to make losses as small as possible and you will be fine.

Some further Advice and Guidance.

STAGS

Why is the acronym STAGS important to us as traders?

Stay in control at all times, have a plan to work with and stick with it.
Timing, know when to get into and out of a trade. Use your plan.
Act quickly, don't wait for the odds to increase or decrease. Plan ahead for the profit or small loss you'll be happy with.
Green up and take your profit straight away. Don't dither and hesitate and lose some or all of it.
Start all over again....

You must plan your trades, there is no other sensible way to trade

It should be obvious by now that having no plan lowers your chances of being successful. On the contrary, having a plan doesn't guarantee success, but it makes it more probable, and that's what we are dealing with, probabilities.

If we do all we can to make sure that the balance of probability is in our favour, the chance of long term profitability is greatly enhanced.

Take your time and decide what you want to do. Find a game and strategy that suits you and your trading style, and is likely to provide you a worthwhile profit.

You can then have every confidence that you have made the very best selections you can and you now have the best strategies to take advantage of it.

There are no guarantees with any selection process though, so prepare for strange things to happen during matches and always be ready to cut a trade short if your capital looks in danger. Trust yourself.

Say that an early goal scuppers your planned LTD1/W1 trade. Move on to the next match on your list. It's not all bad news for your fully researched match. An early goal can lead to backing O2.5 later in the half.

I usually wait in play before opening a position anyway. I prefer to wait for the odds to increase or lower. I like to see how the game is unfolding. Often red cards, early goals, penalties injuries etc can all happen and then I won't open a trade at all. I suggest you do the same.

I take as few risks with my money as is possible. If I've got a tidy profit say 40%+ I'll green up and move on. There's no point in staying in, risking another goal that could wipe out that profit. You don't often see 2 goals in the first half, but it happens, so if you're into an LTD1 trade, get out as soon as the odds to back the draw have settled.

Don't drink and trade, keep your wits about you at all times. Stay alert and look out for any changes that may affect your trade. Be aware that things outside our control can happen and often do. Betfair could go down, so back up with another exchange such as Smarkets or Betdaq. Your internet could drop out so use 4g or some other means to reconnect your phone or tablet etc. Be like a boy scout, be prepared and be ready for the unexpected.

If the in-play stats are showing you that there is a distinct lack of desire from the teams involved, you may decide that you don't want to open a trade at all. When you decide on this and then have your judgement vindicated by the result, then that can be seen as a win and can be as satisfying as profit. Savour these good judgement calls and look back on them when you feel like

getting involved in markets that you know deep down that you shouldn't be. Play a psychological game with yourself, and become fond of sitting out matches and still profiting by not losing.
You will miss out on winning trades, but it can pay to remember the old adage, "it is far better to wish you were in a trade when you aren't, than it is to wish you weren't in a trade when you are".

Missing a winner and a little profit is of absolutely no consequence in the grand scheme of things. There are always plenty more games to play, and more profits to be made. Don't ever be swayed by FOMO, the Fear Of Missing Out.

In any football trade I would never get in before the game starts (unless I am doing some pre-match scalping). I pretty much always get in around the 15-20 minute mark, no matter what the trade is.

This is because I am not trading a football game, I am trading goals, and goals start going in around the 20 minute mark in the average game. So for me that is the optimum time to get in.

So an entry point for me is pretty standard, 15-20 minutes. That makes things pretty simple for me. No matter what the trade I would always look to

get in at that point and sometimes later, I can afford to be flexible using my built in patience and discipline.
And anyway the exit point is more relevant than the entry point.

If for instance I was trading the over 2.5 goals market and at the start of the game the odds were 2.0 I would wait 20 minutes, by which time the odds would be out to at least 2.60 and I would get in then.
If I went in with a 1 point stake and then a goal came at around 30-35 minutes the odds would drop to about 1.50 and I could trade out with around 70% profit no matter how the game ended.
That kind of return for a 10-15 minutes trade is not to be sniffed at.

The big benefit of getting in at around 20 minutes is that I can check the in-play stats, I'm already well armed with the pre match stats, and decide whether I want to play the game at all. If they are not to my liking I will stay out altogether. If I like them I will trade. If they are somewhere in between the two I will stay out too. You will never be short of matches to get involved with, so make sure you are always highly selective and cautious.

Getting out of a trade for a loss and then seeing circumstances change and your losing trade becoming a winning one can be galling. Remind yourself that protecting your bank is the only thing you need to be concerned about. If that is always in the front of your mind, then the probability of eventual profits is increased.

Now I am going to be absolutely blunt here. The word trading is bandied about like it is going out of fashion by countless sites these days and the idea of being a trader seems to appeal to people much more so than saying you are betting or you are a gambler.

Firstly, trading is very, very tough. There are some smart traders out there sitting behind a desk waiting for your cash to enter a market so they can nab it. You need to be that much smarter and faster.

Secondly, you don't need to trade to make money. You CAN make money betting, be it backing or laying on Betfair. There is always a suggestion it is next to impossible or you cannot beat the market on Betfair but I will say that is nonsense. As someone once alluded to on a post, "you need to discover the relevant edge and have a massive backdated amount of information (stats and in play stats) to back it up".

There are numerous trading and betting services out there on the Interweb. Some are very slick with great marketing and flashy websites. Others not so much. Some show results, some don't. Some are actually very good and others have elements which are useful. But the one thing that most have in common is they are purely businesses.
The guys who run these sites make their money from subscriptions or they make profits from affiliate links. It would be rare to find many who run the services and actually bet the selections themselves week in, week out.

If you are a member of a service and are expecting their selections and those selections alone to make you a full time living then it is time to re-assess your thinking. There are no affiliate links in this book.
That isn't my style. I wrote this to try and help you become better at trading, not as a purely money making endeavour.

Looks at your bank as money that has lost its value and won't be missed if it all goes wrong for you. It could be seen as a tuition fee if you like. It is all about learning, reading, researching and putting cash on the line in real time.

Paper trading is fine when starting out and learning the ropes, but it is a whole new experience with cash on the line. If you put all your eggs into this basket, then prepared to drop them a few times.

Exit Strategy's for LTD's, Overs/Under's etc.

First of all, the definition of an exit strategy is: "A predetermined process to reach a satisfactory profit or loss"

Exit points can work both ways. Sometimes they may be used to lock in a profit and other times they can be used to minimise a loss.

Never go into a trade without an idea of when or where you will exit. If you do not have a predetermined exit in mind, you are more likely to let your emotions take over and you will get greedy or hesitant, and that will inevitably lead to an unnecessary loss.

Trading Out for a Small Loss

Most people would find it absurd to trade out for a loss, but in some instances, it's the smart thing to do in order to protect your bank.

There are two ways to trade out for a loss. The first way is to trade out with the same stake as you originally bet with.

For example, you placed a back bet for a home win at 2.1 for £100. Things are going wrong and the home teams price is now at 2.4. To trade out just lay that selection with £100.

1 £30. Draw £0.00. 2 £0.00

Both of these circumstances represent a major reduction from the
£100 that you would lose had you not used this strategy. £30 is significantly better than a ton.

The second method is to equalise a loss. Instead of having a big loss on one selection, the loss will be spread across all 3 selection's.

This is the safer lower loss option because it turns your potential high loss into a predictable and more manageable smaller loss which will help to preserve your bankroll.

To equalise a loss, all you need to do is divide the unequalised loss with the current lay odds and then subtract it from your original stake.

So in our case, we used a lay bet of £87.50 to equalise a loss a loss of £30 to £12.50.

* * *

£30 (original unequalised loss) / 2.4 (current lay odds) = £12.5 =>

£100 − £12.5 = £87.50 (our lay stake). Which in turn will give us.

1 -£12.50

X -£12.50

2 -£12.50

Or you could simply use the cash out button on the exchange or the hedging button if you're using trading software.
So there you have it, some thought's for you to consider. I hope you enjoyed this personal insight into the world of trading. I hear you thinking 'It's not as easy as I thought, so little time and so much to learn'.

So my advice is start slowly, from the beginning. Take all the time you need, take it step by step, make notes, read this book as often as you need. Learning to trade successfully and calmly takes patience, and it's not a sprint, it's a marathon. Make sure you enjoy the process of mastering the markets.

* * *

And never forget, losing less is more important than winning.

Printed in Great Britain
by Amazon